25 Walks in the Finger Lakes Region

D1563559

Chimney Bluff on the Lake Ontario shore (see Walk 11)

25
Walks in the Finger Lakes Region

BILL EHLING

New Hampshire Publishing Company   Somersworth

Acknowledgments

A book like this is written by others, by those with the foresight and dedication to preserve a piece of woodland, plant the seeds that have become today's forest, and construct the footpaths that allow us to walk the hills, glens, and ravines of this region. To all those who have made hiking in the Finger Lakes area such a pleasure and given purpose to this book, my sincerest thanks. I am indebted as well to those who have so ably helped me in the necessary chores of typing and editing: Linda Gorton, Beth Johnson, and Cindy Stultz. I am especially grateful to Catherine Baker, editor, whose support and suggestions were invaluable. I also am indebted to many members of the Finger Lakes Trail Conference who provided information and assistance, especially Ervin Markert, Stephen Weber, Wally Wood, and Mrs. Korby Wade; and to members of Onondaga Chapter of the Adirondack Mountain Club, especially Charlie Embree for his detailed maps. I also thank Olga, who shared with me the excitement of hiking and the long hours of writing so that others might find the same excitement.

An Invitation to the Reader

With time, trails can be rerouted and signs and landmarks altered. If you find that changes have occurred on the routes described in this book, please let us know so that corrections may be made in future editions. The author and publisher also welcome other comments and suggestions. Address all correspondence:

Editor, *25 Walks*
New Hampshire Publishing Company
Box 70
Somersworth, NH 03878

International Standard Book Number: 0-89725-004-4
Library of Congress Catalog Card Number: 78-71718

Published by New Hampshire Publishing Company
Somersworth, New Hampshire 03878

Printed in the United States of America
Photographs by the author except as follows: pages 55, 66, 95, 106, 117, by Nancy-Jane Jackson and page 111 by David Buckman.
Design by Uneeda Design, Inc.

To my children, Teresa, James, and Clare. May the simple legacy of the quietude of a woodland path, a shaft of sunlight in a forest glen, and a hilltop vista be the treasure which, found by them in the past, they can share with theirs in the future.

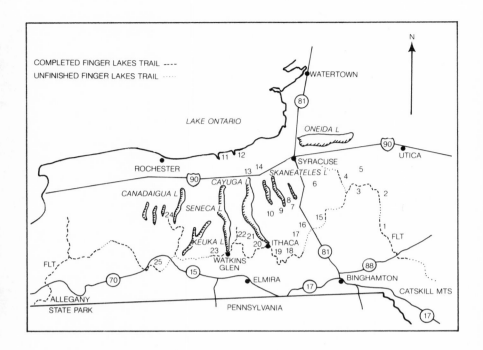

Contents

Trails that are part of the Finger Lakes Trail system are well marked with signs and blazes.

Introduction

The Finger Lakes Region has its own unique charm—
a quality that is easy to recognize and pleasant to
experience, but difficult to capture in a word. When
you encounter this area and walk its hills, it is like a
chance acquaintance with a stranger who you immediately sense will become a long-time friend.

This region is situated approximately midway between
New York City and Niagara Falls. It contains dozens of
major streams and many more large and small lakes.
The six long lakes from which the region derives its
name are, from east to west: Skaneateles, Owasco,
Cayuga, Seneca, Keuka, and Canandaigua. Gouged
and shaped by glaciers, these lakes line up like fingers
on a north-south axis. They lie between Syracuse and
Rochester and extend from a corridor south of Lake
Ontario nearly to the Pennsylvania border. The region
covers more than nine thousand square miles, encom-
passing fourteen counties and including more than
six hundred miles of shoreline and more than five
hundred miles of hiking trails.

This is an area of prosperous-looking farms and
attractive towns, vineyards and pastureland, trout
derbies and flower festivals, museums and historic
homes, summer theatres and religious pageants, boat
cruises and international road races. It contains
almost two score golf courses and more than a dozen
ski centers, as well as twenty-seven colleges and
universities. Yet amidst all these signs of cultivation
and civilization exist vast areas of largely untamed
forest laced with miles of foot trails far removed from
the urban noise and bustle. It is a place of beauty and
wonder, of conventional sights mixed with delightful
contrasts—a land that welcomes the hiker. To walk

over this land is to become familiar with its character-
istics and its geography, much of which is overlooked
if you travel by car.

Some of the region's charm may be found in the
unexpected and paradoxical. For example, to the north
of the Finger Lakes is an east-west corridor through
which once passed the Erie Canal; today it is an
urbanized, industrialized belt that runs from Troy and
Albany in the east through Utica, Syracuse, and
Rochester to Buffalo and Niagara Falls in the west.
A little farther south, however, you find the lake
plains with rich farmlands, fruit farms, vineyards,
and dairy herds; here, in striking juxtaposition, is the
rural landscape.

Still farther south the landscape changes again; you
now come almost unexpectedly to the chain of
highlands and woodlands that runs from the Catskills
on the east to Allegany State Park in the west. And just
south of this virtual wilderness you find, as if to
emphasize the contrast, still another urban belt, the
Binghamton-Elmira-Corning sector.

There is also contrast in the landscape itself. In
general, this is a gentle land of rolling hills and
rounded valleys. Yet nestled in this gentleness is the
rugged grandeur of the deep gorges at Watkins Glen,
Taughannock Falls, Enfield Glen, and Fillmore Glen.
Spectacular waterfalls and soaring walls of stone seem
all the more breath-taking amidst such serenity.

Then there is the region's cultural and historical back-
ground. Indian names like Seneca, Cayuga, Otisco,
and Keuka are evidence of its heritage, as are the
Indian legends and the old Indian trails found in
places like Shindagin Hollow State Forest. These early

inhabitants believed that the Finger Lakes were formed when the Great Spirit placed his hand on the earth indicating the chosen spot.

You also see evidence of a more recent heritage recorded on historical markers that tell you where Indian treaties were signed, generals marched their troops, and famous men and women were born. You see it, too, in the old farms and mills that still stand, and in crumbling foundations, abandoned fields, and unattended stone fences now lost in new forests. The silent story is there; you need but walk and look about you. This land was settled by pioneers in the late 1700s, and by 1900 it had become dotted with farms and growing towns and crisscrossed by roads, turnpikes, and canals. Today, however, it has fewer farms and people than it did one hundred years ago, and untamed forests cover much of the once-cultivated land.

The change is due in part to the region's deep acid soils, high hills, and short growing season, all of which subjected farmers to serious economic difficulties. People have finally abandoned much of the land to seek livelihood elsewhere, and in a relatively short period of thirty-five years—from 1925 to 1960—the harvested acreage here declined 41 percent. Clearly, this is not good cropland.

It was during this period of exodus that the state began its land acquisition program, buying many farms and turning them into state forest, game management regions, and recreational areas. The belt of forests across the lower part of the Finger Lakes Region is really a belt of state land—a rich resource in open spaces.

How to Use This Book

The idea behind this book is to get you to a trailhead so that you can start hiking. The hikes have been clustered into five geographical groupings: East Central, Central, North Central, South Central, and West Central. Most are on county, state, or federal lands, but where they cross private land they are on trails, such as the Finger Lakes Trail, for which permission to hike has already been obtained from the landowners. Hence, you need not be concerned about trespassing on private or posted land.

The trails were selected with variety in mind. Some of them are well known and, therefore, popular. Others are more secluded and lightly traveled. An effort has been made to strike a balance between the better and lesser known hiking areas, while avoiding those that have become tourist meccas. Left out of the book are trails at such popular areas as Letchworth, Watkins Glen, Robert Treman, and Buttermilk Falls. These are spectacular places to see and to hike; however, you do not need this book to find your way to or through them. Their locations are marked on any state map, and maps of their trails can be obtained at the park entrances. However, Bowman Lake State Park has been included because of its variety and the low use of its trails, and I selected Taughannock Falls State Park for its picturesque falls—the highest east of the Rockies—and its lightly traveled upper rim trails. I have also chosen certain little-used hiking areas that adjoin state parks so that the hiker can have the best of both worlds. The hike around Summer Hill, for instance, is by Fillmore Glen, and the Enfield Trail adjoins Robert Treman State Park.

The hikes were designed to allow you to walk a loop and see as much of the countryside as possible without backtracking. An accurate hiking distance is provided at the beginning of each hike's description, as is an estimated hiking time, the accuracy of which will depend on your own walking speed and the number of stops you make along the way. You are invited to shorten any hike that appears too long by simply walking as far as you like and retracing your steps. After all, the object of this book is to help you enjoy your outing, not to turn hiking into an endurance contest.

Also listed at the outset is the Unites States Geological Survey (USGS) quadrangle map or maps covering the area the hike traverses. In all cases, the USGS name refers to the 7.5' series; these quadrangle maps are available usually at local sporting goods stores or directly from the USGS. In some instances other published hiking maps are also noted. All these maps will give you more detailed, although not necessarily as up-to-date, information than the simple sketch maps that accompany the hike descriptions. These sketch maps are meant only to help you visualize the route followed and its location relative to other trails and important features in the landscape. North is at the top; the standard cartographic symbols used throughout this book are as follows:

Paved road ▬   *Parking* →

Dirt road =====   *Point of interest* ✳

Hike route ▬ ▬ ◣

Other trails ....

Lean-to ᅲ

Building ■

The Trails

The hikes in this book lead you along marked and maintained trails as well as into some areas where there are no designated foot trails or trail signs. The major trail system in this region is the Finger Lakes Trail (FLT), which has been constructed and maintained by a host of local hiking groups, each of which is responsible for a relatively short stretch of trail. Though parts of the FLT are not yet finished, much of it can be hiked, and when it is completed it will offer some 650 miles of walking trails in this part of the state.

The main FLT, which runs from Allegany State Park to the Catskills, is blazed with white rectangular markers on trees and fence posts. There are also a number of spur trails attached to the FLT, such as the Interloken Trail and the Onondaga Trail, and these are blazed orange. Most of the other trails in this book are without blazes or markers, but any hiking you do on them is easy and safe since they usually follow dirt roads, jeep trails, or abandoned wagon roads.

While all the walks in this book are meant to be day hikes, about two-thirds of the listed areas can be used by the weekend backpacker. To this end, potential tenting areas, lean-to locations, and areas where camping is restricted or prohibited have been noted where appropriate in the hike descriptions.

I have not classified these trails according to hiking ease or difficulty because such judgments are inevitably subjective. As a general rule, however, they fall into the easy-to-moderate class. A few stretches may prove to be a bit demanding, but most of the trails are relatively level and easy to walk. If you have doubts, bear in mind that a hike's degree of difficulty depends not only on the terrain but also on the distance to be traveled and your physical condition. Remember, too, that weather is a factor, and that rain or snow may increase the difficulty of your walk or hike considerably.

Dress and Equipment

Serious backpackers and mountain climbers require an elaborate array of expensive equipment, but for the hikes in this book you will need little more than some comfortable clothes and a good pair of hiking boots. Of course, the boots are most important, and you should take care to select a pair that will allow you to enjoy these hikes with a minimum of discomfort and fatigue. I have found that a medium weight, over-the-ankle hiking boot is best, and, though they are not cheap, they are certainly a worthwhile investment for anyone who plans to walk more than a few blocks.

You should also bring along a sweater or light jacket, as well as some raingear. With full deference to local weather reports, starting out in the sun does not always guarantee coming back in the sun, and walking in the rain, particularly on a cold day, is no way to enjoy an outing.

Other items you will need are: a plastic water bottle (never assume that stream or lake water is safe to drink), a small first-aid kit, bug dope (in summer), a small G.I.-type can opener, matches, food, sunglasses, a flashlight (with extra cells), a knife, a map, and a compass, as well as a daypack in which to put all of this. And although a pair of binoculars are not essential, they can add much to a hike.

One more thing you may want to bring is a field guide. This will help you to identify much of the flora and fauna you pass on your hike, thereby strengthening the bond that exists between the hiker and the natural environment.

Ski Touring and Snowshoeing

Many of the areas that these hikes traverse are ideal for winter sports, and I have included information pertaining to ski touring and snowshoeing wherever it was appropriate. Virtually all of these areas can be snowshoed or skied (exceptions have been noted), though some are certainly better than others. There are some simple courtesies that should be considered. You can ski where people showshoe without causing problems, but you should not snowshoe on ski touring trails. Snowshoe tracks can destroy a carefully groomed ski trail, and a lack of consideration in this situation may lead to friction between skiers and snowshoers. The Finger Lakes Region receives plenty of snow during the winter months, and its many trails provide ample room for everyone.

Additional Information

Department of Environmental Conservation
50 Wolf Road
Albany, NY 12233

Provides brochures on state forest lands and wildlife management areas and an outdoor recreation guide. County maps, which show the location of state lands, can be obtained from regional DEC offices for $.50 each.

Finger Lakes Association
309 Lake Street
Penn Yan, NY 14527

Issues an annual booklet, "Finger Lakes Regional Travel Guide."

Department of Parks and Recreation
Onondaga County
Onondaga Lake Parkway
Liverpool, NY 13088

Provides brochures, pamphlets, and other literature on the county's forests, parks, and nature center and current listings of seasonal activities.

Finger Lakes Trail Conference, Inc.
12 Corners Branch
Rochester, NY 14618

Provides a guide to the map series for the Finger Lakes Trail system and information about the conference and member hiking clubs.

Finger Lakes State Park and Recreation Commission
Taughannock Falls State Park
R.D. 3
Trumansburg, NY 14886

Offers information and maps for the state parks in the Finger Lakes district.

Division of Tourism
New York State Department of Commerce
99 Washington Avenue
Albany, NY 12245

Issues the New York State highway map and booklets on camping sites and hiking.

1

Bowman Lake

Hiking distance: 9¼ miles
Hiking time: 5 hours
Map: USGS East Pharsalia

If you are looking for a place to mix the conventional
and the more unusual, the state park at Bowman Lake
may be your spot. Here you can choose between trail
hiking or bushwhacking, park camping or wilderness
tenting, lake fishing for trout or pond fishing for
pickerel, and even listening to a chorus of peepers or
taking in a pop concert. And if that isn't enough, there
are swimming and picnicking facilities in addition to
several marked hiking trails, among them a thirty-six
station nature trail, a section of the main Finger Lakes
Trail (FLT), and one of its spurs.

The 660-acre Bowman Lake State Park, located in
Chenango County eight miles west of Oxford, is surrounded by an even larger tract of state forest land,
making the area a remote, woodland retreat. Situated
in a high, plateaulike region marked by low, gently
rolling hills, this vast tract with its relatively level
terrain offers hiking that falls into the easy category.

The route you follow runs from Bowman Lake, on the
west side of the park, north along the main FLT for
2 miles to the Berry Hill fire tower and then returns on
a network of dirt roads that weave through scenic
hardwood and evergreen forests.

The state park makes a fine base for a day or weekend
outing. There are over two hundred tent-trailer sites

The Berry Hill fire tower north of Bowman Lake

nestled beneath lofty shade trees, and for those who prefer a more rugged setting, wilderness camping is permitted in the state forest land outside the park. Particularly pleasant is the area around Whaley Pond, which you pass on your return leg.

This is an ideal spot in the summer or early fall. If the day is warm, cool off after your walk with a dip in Bowman Lake, or, if you are in the fishing mood and equipped with tackle, try your luck with the lake's trout. The rainbows can run in the two-pound class. The Art-in-the-Park Festival, a musical series that is free for park guests, operates during August and early September. As with all state parks, there is a small vehicular use charge.

Access. Bowman Lake State Park is located off NY 220 between Oxford and McDonough. From the east and south, travel NY 12 to Oxford and then NY 220 west 8 miles to the park; from Cortland follow NY 41 south to Smithville Flats and then NY 220 east through McDonough.

Trail. The white-blazed FLT, which has its beginning ten miles to the south by the Chenango River, follows the main park road to the southernmost parking area by the lake. Leave your car here and follow the blazes as they head north along the lake. Until recently this thirty-five-acre, spring-fed pond was only a large marsh drained by a small stream. In 1960 the state's Department of Environmental Conservation acquired the land and a year later completed construction of a dam that formed the lake.

When you reach the wooded area on the far side of the northernmost parking area, a sign for the FLT directs you into the woods. The trail snakes right and then left before heading north. One mile from the lake you come into the open to cross Leslie Simpson Road (dirt) and then you re-enter the woods. The walk here is level and pleasant and cool during the summer. Another mile brings you to a more open area where you may find cows grazing or resting in the shade. Continue on the trail until it turns right and emerges in a field. A short walk through the field and up small Berry Hill brings you to the state-operated fire tower and a small house used by the observer when on duty. You can climb this tower even when it is not manned. From the top you can see about twenty or thirty miles in every direction. The surrounding land, most of it state-owned, is virtually all tree covered; only a few farms can be spotted in the distance. To the north is a vast tract known as the New Michigan State Forest, and still further north, the state's Pharsalia Game Management Area.

On your return route you follow roads that lead through heavily wooded state land. In summer, it is best to walk them in the early morning or late afternoon, when the tall trees lining them cast the greatest shadows. From the fire tower, follow the narrow dirt road east about ¼ mile to Tower Road. Turn right and take this dirt lane south 1½ miles to Leslie Simpson Road. Turn right onto this road, which you crossed earlier, and follow it 1½ miles to another dirt lane, Whaley Road, on your left.

Turn left onto Whaley Road and walk about ⅓ mile to a narrow dirt road that forks left. Follow it ½ mile to Whaley Pond, an impoundment about the same size as Bowman Lake, but where pickerel, not trout, hold sway. (If you are in the mood and equipped with a USGS topographical map and a compass, you can bushwhack directly east from here to reach the section of the FLT you walked at your start. The land is flat and forested and the distance just a shade over ½ mile.)

Retrace your steps to Whaley Road and continue walking south. Soon the road turns sharply right, winding its way for the next 1 mile through tall, well-spaced red spruce. This section is especially attractive for hiking.

You finally intersect an unmarked dirt road. Turn left (east) and follow it ¼ mile to Sherman Road, on the left just past a right bend. Bear left onto this dirt road. After about 1 mile, just after you start down a small hill, a dirt lane comes up on your right. The white blazes on trees alongside it indicate that you have intercepted the southern leg of the FLT.

Follow the white blazes to the left, walking north about 50 yards. You are now at the outlet end of Bowman Lake. From here it is a short walk back along the eastern edge of the lake to your car or campsite.

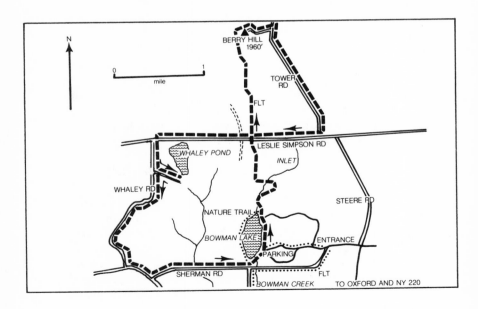

If you have time for an additional 1½-mile-long jaunt, follow the orange blazes of the FLT spur trail around the west side of Bowman Lake. This is the nature trail; a self-guiding pamphlet to use at the stations is available from the park office at the entrance.

Winter activities. Each January a cross-country race is held at the park, a good indication that this is fine ski touring country. Special trails are marked for skiing, among them the FLT. The park is open all year, allowing snow camping for snowmobilers, ski tourers, and snowshoers during the winter.

2
McDermott Hill

Hiking distance: 8 miles
Hiking time: 4 hours
Map: USGS South Otselic

The charm of this place is its unpretentiousness. A tract of state land east of Cortland, it is unofficially known as McDermott Hill. It is just a forested hilltop where you can hike quietly along a section of the Finger Lakes Trail (FLT).

Yet as the poet Ezra Pound noted, "Learn of the green world what can be thy place." Perhaps you will find this small hilltop such a green world, for the pleasure of walking is somehow heightened here. In spring, when the trees put on the season's first yellow-green dress, it becomes a delight of renewal. In summer it turns into a cathedral of green coolness. In autumn, amidst the fall foliage of yellows and reds, it evokes a wistful memory of summer gone.

Here, as with some other areas along the FLT, there are problems of map names and official designation. The state Lands and Forest Division uses a technical, intra-departmental name: Chenango 20. An earlier and less technical label given this same area by the state is Bucks Brook State Forest, although no one around here ever uses this title. The map published by the Finger Lakes Trail Conference calls the hilltop over which the FLT runs McDermott Hill, making this the popular name. It is also the name used in this book. However, if you are using a recent USGS quadrangle map you will find no McDermott Hill listed, nor will you find any indication that this is even state land. Finally, although most state forests have special name signs posted along the roadways through them, you should be aware that you will find no such signs here. To the average person passing this forest, it is simply a quiet wooded place.

The suggested loop, which follows a completed section of the FLT out and dirt roads back, is a good day's hike. It takes you through an inviting stand of hardwoods and evergreens, over quietly flowing, sun-flecked brooks, through a small gorge, and to a hilltop from

View from McDermott Hill

which you can see the surrounding countryside stretching away in all directions. And should you wish to spend the night, there is an ideal campsite in a partial clearing near McDermott Hill. During the day this fern swale is warmed by shafts of sunlight, and during the night it collects and holds the soft talk of the night peepers.

When you walk, do so slowly; this wooded area is host to a great number of mushrooms, and if you look carefully along the path's edges, you may see, as I did, an impressive variety on a day's walk. Watch for the various amanitas, collybias, galerninas, pholiotas, russulas, and polypores, especially *polyporus versicolor*, or "turkey tails." Bring along your mushroom field guide; it makes identification easier and more fun.

Access. This state forest lies between DeRuyter and South Otselic. From DeRuyter, take the DeRuyter Turnpike south 3 miles to the top of the hill where Ridge Road (dirt) cuts off on your right. Follow Ridge Road 1.5 miles to Ratville Road, another dirt road. Past the second house (and barn) Ratville Road narrows to a single lane. One mile from that point, you should encounter trail markers—hand-lettered words painted on trees on both sides of the road—for the McDermott Hill section of the FLT. Park in the small area off the road just beyond.

Trail. Turn left (southeast) onto the FLT. It leads you uphill through the woods for ½ mile, and then, on more level terrain, gradually loops to the left (north). After ¼ mile, it turns right (east) and a short distance beyond brings you to Ridge Road. Walk to the right (south) for about 25 yards to pick up the trail on the other side. Soon after you re-enter the woods, you slant downhill and cross a small stream. This is Bucks

Brook, which flows south and eventually empties into the Otselic River just below the hamlet of Seventh Day Hollow.

From here the trail moves uphill through evergreens that soon give way to maples and beeches. At the crest the land flattens, indicating that you are now walking a ridge. Soon you enter a stand of tall, well-spaced red spruce, one of the several attractive areas in this forest.

The trail now swings gradually to your right and heads south. Soon it pitches downward, taking you into a small gully where in spring a brook flows eastward. In summer the gully is usually dry. The trail leads up the other side to another level. On your right is the area's highest point (el. 1,860'), designated as McDermott Hill on the FLT map.

You soon come to a partial clearing filled with ferns. If you are planning to camp overnight, this may be the place you will want to stay.

Continuing south ½ mile, you begin a gradual descent. Within the next ½ mile the slope steepens, and as you near the trail's end the downward pitch becomes quite pronounced. The FLT terminates on Bucks Brook Road (dirt) in a modest-sized gorge called Seventh Day Hollow. The gorge's vertical sides are exposed shale, and its bottom is just wide enough to accommodate the road and Buck's Brook. The creek bed and exposed sites by the road's side are good places to search for fossils.

Now turn right on Bucks Brook Road and head north. Following the twists and turns of the brook, the road ascends gradually, rising out of the gorge into a ravine and then into a wider-bottomed hollow. One mile from the trail's end, you emerge from the woods; fields spread off to your right along the lower side of McDermott Hill. You soon re-enter another wooded section from which you emerge in ¼ mile. A short climb up a small, open hill brings to Ridge Road. If you wish to shorten your hike, you can turn right (north) now and head back toward your vehicle.

The hike, however, continues left (south) on Ridge Road to a fine overlook. You reach the summit of Cary Hill (el. 1,957') in ¾ mile. The wooded areas on both sides prevent you from enjoying any vistas though, so walk another mile to the ridge's next high point. Here fields on both sides of the road allow you fine views of rolling hills to the east and west.

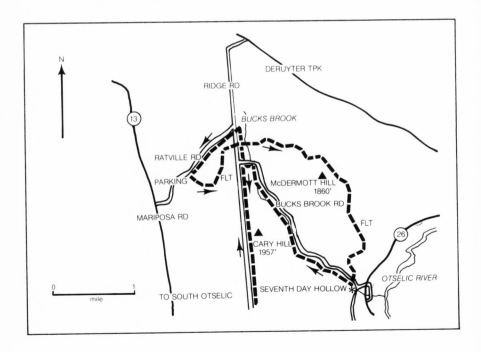

When ready, turn around and walk back along Ridge Road, past the intersection of Bucks Brook Road and, ¼ mile beyond, to the FLT crossing. Turn left here. Another ½ mile brings you to Ratville Road and back to your vehicle.

Winter activities. You are in good ski touring and snowshoeing country. The snows come often and stay on the ground long, especially in the forest. Ridge Road is plowed in winter, allowing you access to the FLT, the northern end of which is ideal for ski touring. The southern section from McDermott Hill to Bucks Brook Road is too steep, however, to negotiate on skis.

3
Cuyler Hill
State Forest

Hiking distance: 7¾ miles
Hiking time: 4½ hours
Maps: USGS Cuyler; FLT "Randall Hill"

It is not always easy to put a name to a hike. This one could be called the Randall Hill hike, since it takes you over Randall Hill, a seven-mile-long ridge northeast of Cortland. I have preferred to call it the Cuyler Hill hike, after the thickly wooded state forest that runs almost the full length of that high but relatively level ridge. Whatever the name, it is your introduction to an area that can quickly become a favorite for both day hikes and overnight backpacking.

Here you walk the well-marked Randall Hill section of the Finger Lakes Trail (FLT), which was constructed and is maintained by the Onondaga Chapter of the Adirondack Mountain Club. Running along the flattened crest of Randall Hill, making for easy-to-moderate walking, the trail meanders through tall, well-spaced hardwoods, stands of evergreens, swales of ferns, and cool glens with quietly flowing brooks. It is the central portion of a 21-mile stretch of maintained and marked trails in this part of New York state; to the south the FLT leads a little over 10 miles to Mount Roderick near Solon and to the northwest, about 11 miles to NY 26 near Otselic Center.

The loop recommended here is only 7¾ miles long and includes a short detour to a lean-to and a scenic overlook.

Access. To reach Cuyler Hill for the start of this hike, drive to Cuyler, a hamlet of two dozen homes slightly off NY 13. In the center of the hamlet, turn onto Lincklean Road and drive east for 2 miles to Cuyler Hill Road, on the right just beyond a small, two-story white house. Turn here and drive uphill for 1.1 miles to a cluster of farm buildings where the paved road intersects a dirt one. Turn left onto the dirt road (a continuation of Cuyler Hill Road) and drive .4 mile to Stoney Brook Road, the first dirt road on the left. Continue uphill on this road. At .3 mile you reach woods and the edge of Cuyler Hill State Forest. If you stop here and look back, you have a wide vista of long valleys, pastureland, and wooded hilltops. Two miles to the west rises Pease Hill and farther west, the Morgan and Truxton hills (see Walk 4).

Overlooks across farm fields offer fine views of rolling hills

Continuing another .2 mile, watch for the word Hike painted in white on a tree to your right. This is where the Randall Hill section of the FLT crosses the road. Park your vehicle here.

Trail. Begin your walk by following the trail south, downhill into the forest. Within a few feet you come to several trail signs—white lettering painted on a large tree on the left—that read Cuyler Summit 1 mi, Rose Hollow 2½ mi, and Randall Hill Rd 3 mi. The trail markers along the main FLT are white; those on spur trails, orange.

In about ½ mile the trail passes over what in spring and early summer is Bundy Creek, though by late summer it may be a dry stream bed. Another ½ mile brings you to Cuyler Summit, the high point (el. 2,080') of Randall Hill. Beyond it, the trail is relatively flat for a stretch before starting a gradual descent. In about ½ mile, after making a sharp left turn and then one to the right, you see an orange-marked spur trail forking to your left. This leads to Elwood Road, a dirt lane running parallel to the main trail. Continue on the main trail for another ¾ mile, through several fern swales, over another high point, called Kiwi Summit (el. 2,020') on the FLT map, and finally to a second spur to Elwood Road. Shortly the main trail passes over a third high point, called Accordion Summit (el. 2,020') on the FLT map.

About ¼ mile beyond, the trail forks. Here, painted on a tree, a white-lettered sign reads Rose Hollow with an arrow pointing right. Bearing right and following the orange-blazed spur trail downhill for ¼ mile, you come to the Rose Hollow Lean-to, which overlooks a small gully cut by Enz Brook. Near the lean-to look for two signs hand-lettered on trees: one directs you to an overlook to the southwest; the other to a spring. It is a short walk to the overlook, but in summer the vista is restricted by the full-foliaged trees. Try the spring trail for some refreshing, cold water and a much better view. In ⅛ mile it leads you across the brook to the small spring, which is productive even in summer, and the trail's end. But if you bear left and walk another 100 feet through the woods you step into a field, where you have an excellent view of the distant, wooded tops of Seacord and Allen hills.

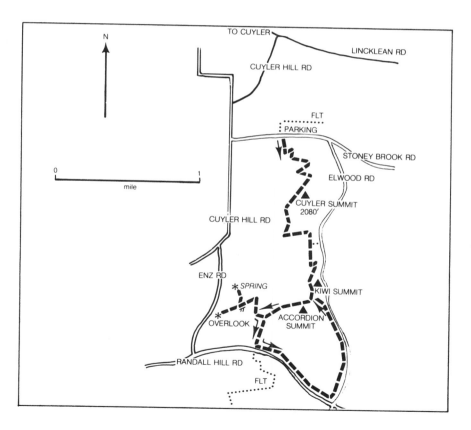

Retrace your steps to the main trail, turn right, and continue walking south. The trail now pitches gradually downhill and brings you ¼ mile through large stands of maples and smaller stands of evergreens to Randall Hill Road. The FLT heads across the road and into the forest, but to continue your hike, turn left and walk this road for 1 mile, until it intersects Elwood Road. At the corner on your right you can see a clearing with makeshift fireplaces. This camping area is one of several spots, along with the lean-to, where you can stay on an overnight outing.

Turn left on Elwood Road and walk another 1 mile to the orange markers and Hike sign that indicate the entrance to one of the spur trails you passed on your way out. Turn left here and walk the short distance (1,000 feet) back to the main trail, where you turn right (north). You are now 2¼ miles south of your starting point. In less than an hour you should be back on Stoney Brook Road where you left your vehicle.

Winter activities. This place is ideal for ski touring and snowshoeing. The main trail has enough variation in terrain to make skiing interesting and is long enough to allow you to ski all day. Since the roads in the state forest are not plowed in winter, they too can be used for touring. The snowfall is heavy here and the forest holds it well to the end of March, and sometimes into early April.

4

Morgan Hill
State Forest

Hiking distance: 9½ miles
Hiking time: 5 hours
Map: USGS Tully

Like the persons for whom they were named, Fellows
Hill, Jones Hill, and Morgan Hill are nextdoor neigh-
bors, and they comprise a varied and delightful hiking
terrain. Spread over these three hills, all of which are
about 2,000 feet in elevation, are 5,508 acres of state
land. Officially, this area is called Morgan Hill State
Forest, though locally it is known variously as Fabius
Forest, Morgan Hill, or Shackham Woods.

Through this state land and over some adjoining
private land runs the Onondaga Trail. Designed,
marked, and maintained by members of the Onondaga
Chapter of the Adirondack Mountain Club, it consti-
tutes one of the spur trails to the Finger Lakes Trail
(FLT) system. This trail is well groomed and marked
with orange blazes painted on trees.

The entire Morgan Hill State Forest area is covered
with trees, of which about 70 percent are in pine and
spruce plantations; the other 30 percent are natural
hardwoods. In the middle of the forest there is even a
section of virgin timber several hundred years old. You
will find some fine overlooks here, as well as magnificent Tinker Falls, a pond stocked with brook trout,
an Adirondack-type lean-to, a rushing wilderness
brook, and a series of hills, gullies, and ravines to add
variety to your hike. In short, the Morgan Hill area is a
hiker's delight.

Access. You begin your hike in the Morgan Hill State Forest by entering the Onondaga Trail at Spruce Pond, a small impoundment just .2 mile southwest of Fellows Hill, where the dirt road forks to the left. (The pond is not shown on the USGS map as it was created after the map was last updated.)

Spruce Pond, in turn, can be reached from I-81 by exiting at Tully (about halfway between Syracuse and Cortland) and then heading east on NY 80. Just beyond the hamlet of Apulia, look for Herlihy Road, a hard-packed, two-lane dirt road. Turn right onto it; in 1.2 miles you reach Morgan Hill State Forest, marked by the end of farm fields and the beginning of woods.

Across a farm field to the Morgan, Fellow, and Jones hills

From this point another .7 mile brings you to a fork. Take the one-lane dirt road to your right and drive about .1 mile past a stand of evergreens to a parking area by the dam at the south end of Spruce Pond. Leave your car here.

You will notice that this area is used for picnicking and camping, and if your interests include fishing, you can try the pond for "natives," the beautiful red-spotted brook trout stocked by the state.

Trail. On a tree near the parking area is painted the word Hike and an arrow pointing across the dam. On the other side, a second sign indicates the beginning of the trail. Follow the trail halfway around the pond and then to the left up a relatively short but sharp hill.

Where the orange-marked trail reaches the crest it flattens out and heads west. In about five minutes you start a gradual descent that brings you to a large stand of smooth-barked beeches. Beyond this point the trees become smaller and gradually thin out as you enter what was once a field, now taken over by saplings and evergreens. Here you are hiking on private land and will continue to do so for the next mile.

You soon leave the field and enter a stand of trees that shades an unused wagon trail and a small brook that flows southward to Tinker Falls. After crossing the brook, you pass through another abandoned field before re-entering the woods. The trail wanders a bit here and then brings you to the summit of Jones Hill.

Your path now descends sharply for about 100 feet. To your immediate right an opening through the trees offers you the first vista—a grand view of Truxton Valley to the south and Labrador Hollow to the north.

The drop-off at the overlook is an abrupt and breath-taking 700 feet. Below you lies the half-mile-long Labrador Pond, a "kettle" lake left behind by the retreating glacier thousands of years ago that is tucked in a narrow valley between Jones and Labrador hills. A little to your right, the valley—called Labrador Hollow—fans out to the north around and beyond the hamlet of Apulia Station. Still further north you see a series of smaller hills covered with crop fields and pastureland. The valleys between the ridges were scoured out by the moving glacier.

The trail continues for about 1 mile along the ridge of Jones Hill before beginning a slight descent to a brook. In early spring this brook is high but by midsummer it may be nothing more than a trickle. Turn right and follow the path to Tinker Falls, where the water plunges some twenty feet off a limestone ledge. The falls are a pleasant sight at all times, but they are most impressive in spring when the brook is running heavy with meltwater.

From Tinker Falls continue south along the ridge for another ½ mile. You now begin a descent, with the trail switching back and forth until it emerges on Shackham Road, a well-maintained, two-lane dirt road 470 feet below the ridge crest. The trail crosses this road and drops sharply for 80 feet to Shackham Brook, a picture-book scene in spring and early summer when its water flows over rocks and boulders, forming riffles and small pools en route through the ravine past large stands of pines and hardwoods.

Cross the brook and follow the trail along the edge of the ravine on your right. You climb fairly steeply for a little better than ½ mile, at which point you come to a lean-to and stone fireplace. This is an ideal place to stop for a breather and if you have planned a camping trip, it can be your overnight shelter.

Continue uphill for another ¼ mile to Morgan Hill Road, a one-lane dirt road. Follow the trail across the road about 800 feet to the fire tower (no longer in use). You are now at the summit of Morgan Hill (el. 2,000'), an excellent place to relax in the shade of the hard-woods and evergreens that surround the tower.

Retrace your steps across Morgan Hill Road and down-hill past the lean-to to Shackham Road. Turn right and continue north for 2 miles to the first intersection.

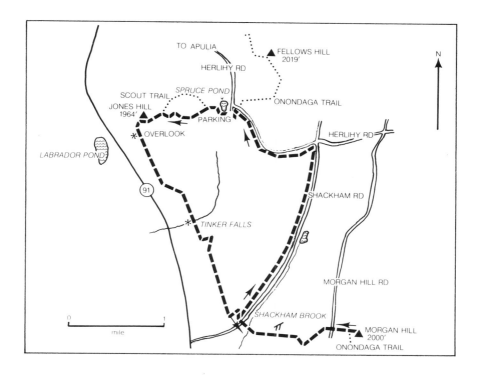

Here Herlihy Road crosses Shackham Road. Turn left onto Herlihy Road and head uphill. After a gentle climb of ¼ mile the road, canopied by trees, flattens out, and it is an easy 1½-mile hike back to Spruce Pond and your car.

Winter activities. This is an excellent and popular place to ski or snowshoe. Only Shackham Road is plowed, but this is sufficient to give you access to the Onondaga Trail, as well as to a number of others. The roads that are unplowed are used extensively by snow-mobilers, but they can be skied to get to Spruce Pond and the Onondaga Trail, which offers challenging—and sometimes difficult—skiing. There is snow cover from late November to early April, and the conditions in January and February are excellent.

5
Highland Forest

Hiking distance: 4½ miles
Hiking time: 2½ hours
Maps: USGS DeRuyter; park map

This 2,700-acre county park sits astride Arab Hill (el. 1,940') in the high land south of Syracuse. As you enter the park and just before reaching the parking lot, you are treated to a vista of rolling hills, woodlands, and farmlands, for Highland Forest is the high point of the region, overlooking the lower lands to the north.

With its almost Adirondack-like appearance and its network of walking trails, fire lanes, and truck trails, Highland Forest is ideal for the hiker. It also is used for horseback riding, and the county maintains riding trails and provides a corral. Near the parking lot there are facilities for picnicking and a softball diamond. During the winter months the forest is a mecca for cross-country skiers, for it offers some of the finest maintained public trails in central New York.

The Onondaga County Parks and Recreation Department has developed an excellent system of hiking trails in this large forest tract. Highland boasts four hiking trails, all of which form loops that begin and end at the parking lot at the northern end of the forest. The "A" loop is just short of a mile long and takes only thirty minutes to walk. The "B" loop runs just over a mile and takes forty minutes; the "C" loop, at 2¾ miles, takes 2½ hours, and the Main Trail, at 8¼ miles, takes 5 to 6 hours. The forest also has a number

There are no views from Highland's highest point

of interconnecting jeep trails, truck roads, and fire lanes which allow enterprising day hikers to make up an endless variety of hikes to suit their own interests and timetables.

To introduce you to many of the park's attractions in an outing of reasonable length, the route described here travels for some distance on each of the four maintained hiking trails and on some of the many jeep and truck lanes. This is a day-use area, so don't plan on camping out. Overnight camping is restricted to organized groups, such as the Scouts, and only then by reservation. If you alter the route described here, be sure to return to your car before dark.

Access. Highland Forest is located south of Syracuse and east of Tully, just off NY 80. From the village of Fabius travel east on NY 80 for 2.2 miles until you see a sign on the left reading Highland Forest that directs you to the right onto the paved Highland Park Road. After making the turn, drive uphill for 1.1 miles to the parking area, on your right, opposite a cluster of buildings: the Community House (in winter a warming hut for cross-country skiers), the park office, and the Pioneer Museum, housing a collection of farm implements, home furnishings, books, and other items of rural life in Onondaga County in the 1800s and early 1900s.

Trail. The trailhead is on the far side of the parking area, next to an information booth and map board. Both a mimeographed guide to the "A" loop, which doubles as a nature trail, and a scaled contour map, showing all the trails, roads, and fire lanes, may be obtained at the park office. The trail system is well-marked; look for the stylized yellow pine tree design painted on trees.

Starting at the information booth, you enter the woods
on the "A" loop and cross a footbridge over one of the
several small brooks you come to on your hike;
together these streams make up the headwaters of the
Tioughnioga River, which flows south through
Cortland and Binghamton en route to the
Susquehanna River.

Beyond the bridge the trail winds through hardwood
for ¼ mile and enters an evergreen stand. This is a
good place to test your skill at tree identification, so
bring your field guide. Many of the trees throughout
the forest are man-planted, and the variety is most
impressive. Among the evergreens are red, white,
Ponderosa, pitch, jack, sugar, and lodgepole pine;
white, Norway, Engleman, and blue spruce; Douglas
and balsam fir; and white cedar. Among the hardwoods
are American basswood, quaking aspen, white ash,
black cherry, yellow birch, American beech, paper
birch, sugar maple, northern red oak, and red maple.

A short distance into the evergreens, you reach a set of
signs; two point left for the Nature Trail and Picnic
Area and one points right for the Main Trail. The "A"
loop returns to the parking area by way of the Nature
Trail.

You continue on the Main Trail. In about 400 feet a
sign points left to the "B" loop, which also returns
directly to the parking area. Stay with the Main Trail.
A few hundred feet further you cross a dirt road and
enter a stand of white and red pines, which soon give
way to hardwoods.

The trail now runs due south, parallel to a gully on your
left, which becomes deeper as you walk south. After 1
mile the trail begins to descend more sharply, finally

turning left into the gully at a point where two brooks merge. After swinging back and forth across the water three times on footbridges, the trail winds up a slight incline to intersect a truck road.

Bear left on the truck road, still heading uphill. By now you have passed over an area that fifty years ago was farmland. The county in 1930 acquired its first parcel of land from two farmers, and with that purchase Highland Forest was founded. During the next three years of the Great Depression the county obtained nine more farms, and by 1935 it had acquired two additional parcels to make up 90 percent of what is now the forest.

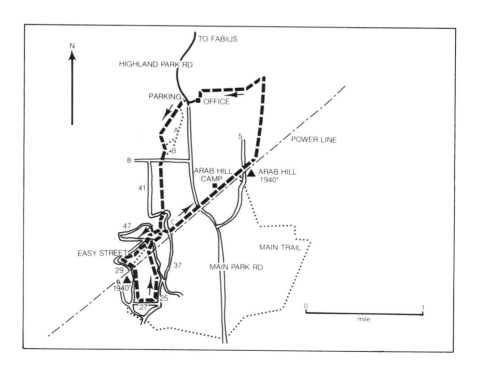

You soon reach a sign marking the place where the "C" loop and the Main Trail diverge. The "C" loop continues on the truck road but the Main Trail, which is still your route, heads to the right and downhill into a gully. The small brook at the bottom drops into a much deeper ravine on your right.

Here a sign points right to Easy Street and left to Goat Trail. Unless you like hard climbing, stay on Easy Street, which swings right out of the gully and makes a sharp left up a moderate ¼-mile incline. At the top the trail takes you out of the woods, across a power-line cut, and back into the forest again. The trail levels out 1,000 feet beyond the cut and a sign informs you that you have reached the "Highest Point in the Forest, 1,940 feet." Continuing, you soon begin a gradual descent. The trail, here a truck road, bends left (east) and shortly encounters a jeep trail with a marker on the right-hand corner. (The jeep and truck trails are numbered, not named.) The corner marker has two numbers: 27, which is the road you have been walking, and 25, which runs in front of you. An arrow also points left to the park office. Following the arrow, keep left on Road 25 for 1,500 feet until it intersects Road 29. Turn left and head uphill; in ¼ mile it brings you back to the power-line cut. Cross it and re-enter the woods, where you will see another sign to the Goat Trail. Take this trail, which leads downhill to the brook you crossed earlier. Retrace your route back to the truck road, turn right, walk about 50 feet to the power-line cut. You are now back on the "C" loop.

Turn left and follow the trail on the power-line cut for ½ mile to the main park road. Turn left and walk 50 feet to a sign pointing right for Arab Hill Camp, one of the camp buildings here used by the Scouts. If you like, you can shorten your hike by following the main park road ½ mile back to the parking area.

The hike continues, however, to the right up the truck road. You pass the Arab Hill Camp, go around a road barrier, and head uphill for ¼ mile before intersecting another stretch of the Main Trail, which has been running north on Road 5.

At this point the Main Trail turns off Road 5 to follow the power line for about 1,000 feet before bearing left into the forest again. Stay on the Main Trail, which now runs north for ½ mile and then loops back, running southwest for ¼ mile and then due west for another ¼ mile, bringing you back to the park office and your start.

Winter activities. This area is a ski tourer's delight. There are four groomed and maintained trails designed for novice through advanced, and the snows come early and stay late—usually into the end of March. Both the park road and parking lot are plowed.

6
Heiberg Forest and Truxton Hill

Hiking distance: 5 miles
Hiking time: 2½ hours
Maps: USGS Tully; USGS Truxton

"Variety" is probably the best single word to describe the Heiberg Forest area, for here you will find a diverse network of trails, fire lanes, and dirt roads to hike, as well as many vistas and overlooks and an assortment of ponds that hold numerous species of gamefish. You will also find a self-guided nature trail that is a delight to walk, and a series of trails that lead you through large stands of hardwoods and into the territory of several herds of whitetail deer. From here you may emerge into an area of thick overgrowth, the ideal habitat of the ruffed grouse for which this forest is well known. There is even a relatively large tract (off-limits) set aside for the study of the blacktail deer, imported from Utah, and a pond used to observe the feeding behavior of the rainbow trout.

The 3,780-acre Heiberg Forest is located atop Truxton Hill (el. 2,020'), a wide, flat ridge that overlooks the towns of Tully, to the north, and Truxton, to the southwest. At first glance, it looks like many other state reforestation areas—but a bit tidier, perhaps. The difference is in its use, for this is an outdoor classroom and experimental station used by the students and faculty of the State University of New York College of Environmental Science and Forestry. Officially it is designated as the "Tully Campus, Heiberg Memorial Forest." Nevertheless, the touches of civilization are

The footpaths at Heiberg take you across land that was farmed as recently as the 1930s

few, limited to the resident forest manager's home and adjacent truck garage and, farther down the road, a small house with several outbuildings that provide shelter for the western blacktail deer.

When you hike Heiberg Forest, you are walking through biological time and succession as the land returns to its natural state. First settled by pioneers in the late 1700s, the area was changed from virgin forest to farmland. However, the soil proved to be highly acidic and poorly drained, and by the 1840s the farmers had turned to lumbering to supplement their incomes and supply the growing demand for fuel created by railroad engines. This only added to the region's economic difficulties, because quality timber soon became scarce and the fast water runoff on the naked land made farming more and more unfeasible. Between 1870 and 1925, two-thirds of the population left the area, and the fields that had been so painfully cleared began to revert to hardwoods. Conifers were planted later when the state began to purchase land in the 1930s.

As you walk, look about for evidence of these transitions—the succession from wilderness to farmland to wilderness. You may find old stone fences running through the forest, traces of old wagon roads, barbed wire embedded in old trees, and mature forest in areas where crops once grew.

Access. Heiberg Forest and Truxton Hill can be reached from Tully, south of Syracuse and just off I-81. From the center of Tully, drive east on NY 80 for .1 mile and turn right onto Railroad Street. At the end of the block, bear left across the railroad tracks onto Grove Street, which soon becomes West Hill Road. Continue uphill on West Hill Road for 1.8 miles. When you reach the hilltop, look back. You have a fine vista of Tully, the wide, north-south Tully valley, and the Tully Lakes, a cluster of fifteen large and small "kettle lakes" formed by the retreating glacier thousands of years ago.

Here also a dirt road, Maple Ridge Road (Truxton Hill Road on the USGS map) forks to the right, and a sign on the left informs you that you are entering Heiberg Forest. In .3 mile you come to a sign on your right announcing the Nature Trail, which you are invited to walk.

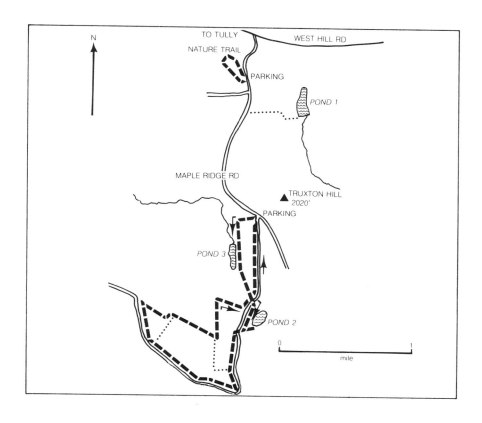

Another .4 mile brings you to a sign for Pond 1; the ½-mile lane to the pond also makes a pleasant walk. Continue another .7 mile down Maple Ridge Road, past the forest manager's house and the sheds housing the blacktail deer to a fork. On your left is a small parking area; leave your vehicle here.

Trail. Start your hike by following the right fork for 100 feet to a sign pointing to Pond 3. Pick up the footpath by the sign and follow it downhill past a large stand of white cedars. At the base of the hill, the trail turns left, running along the forest edge for ¼ mile. On your right are open fields; ahead you can see Pond 3, which is stocked with rainbow trout. You may fish here, but, since the pond is used in field tests, you must obtain a permit from the forest manager. You will find the rainbows big and sassy whether you fly fish or spin cast.

Continue past the pond to a dirt road. Turn right and walk south about ½ mile to another sign, which points to Pond 2. It is a short walk to this pond. All Heiberg's ponds are open to fishing, and they are also used by the deer as watering holes and by ducks and geese in the fall as resting and feeding places.

Return to the dirt road and continue walking south, heading uphill. When you reach the top you have an overlook to the south. The road now bends to the right, gradually arcing to the west and then the north. A mile from the overlook the road starts to descend. On your right is an unmarked fire lane. Bear right, onto the fire lane which runs straight in a southeast direction for ¼ mile, turns left and then right, and again heads in a straight line downhill. Halfway down it intersects a fire lane. Turn left here and follow the fire lane. In ½ mile it turns and heads downhill to intersect the road you walked earlier.

The walk through this section of Heiberg is most pleasant. The fire lanes are broad, clean, and canopied by tall trees. When you reach the dirt road, turn left and walk back to your vehicle. On both sides of you are stately cedars, giving a special charm to this last stretch. The road ascends gradually and then flattens out as you near your vehicle.

Winter activities. Here the terrain is varied, with small hills and level stretches—just the kind of landscape ski tourers love—and the snow comes early, packs well, and stays deep. The forest is laced with ski touring trails, and for the snowshoer there are miles of woodland trails to walk. Maple Ridge Road is plowed as far as the forest manager's house, giving you easy access to all the key trails.

7
Hewitt State Forest

Hiking distance: 3 miles
Hiking time: 1½ hours
Maps: USGS Homer; USGS Otisco Valley

Compared to most other state reforestation areas, Hewitt State Forest is small, covering only about two square miles of hardwoods and evergreens. Nevertheless, it is a delight to hike, primarily because you can walk a natural loop in just over an hour and because it is so rarely used. Except during deer hunting season, you will generally have this little forest to yourself.

This area offers some excellent vistas, for it sits astride the highland overlooking Skaneateles Lake to the northwest, Otisco Lake to the north, and the Tully Lakes to the east. If you look northeast from a high point on the northern edge of the forest, you see Preble Hill a mile away and Gifford Hill two miles away, both 1,800 feet high. Two miles to the south is Brake Hill, which, like the crest you are standing on, reaches an elevation of 1,860 feet. Some local people refer to this high point in the state forest as Hewitt Hill, but officially it has no name.

Access. Hewitt State Forest is most easily reached by following NY 41 to the village of Scott, which is 9 miles north of Homer and 20 miles south of Skaneateles. From the crossroad in the center of Scott, head north on NY 41 for .9 mile to arrive at Hewitt Road, on your right. Turn here and head east. A few hundred feet from NY 41 you pass over Grout Brook, which flows

Stone walls and apple trees—evidence of former farmlands

south through Scott and beyond before turning north
to empty into Skaneateles Lake. It is one of the famous
trout streams of central New York; during spring,
rainbow trout leave the lake and swim up the brook
to spawn.

After crossing Grout Brook, Hewitt Road becomes a
two-lane, hard-packed dirt road. Drive 1 mile to the
first crossroad, turn right, and drive south .7 mile.
Here you will see a little-used jeep trail entering the
forest on your left. Park your vehicle by the side of the
road and begin your walk.

Trail. Enter the woods, following the jeep trail due east.
This trail is unmarked, and although the forest is not
large you should bring a compass and map. For nearly
¼ mile you walk a course due east past an old stone
fence, a reminder that this area was once farmland,
perhaps as recently as fifty to seventy-five years ago,
when the fields were separated by the stones
unearthed during spring plowing. The trail you are
walking is an abandoned wagon road, which now
turns to your right. After a short distance it turns left,
heading you gradually downhill in an easterly direction.

In another hundred feet or so, the trail turns left
(north); in five minutes you find it bending slightly to
the right, taking you downhill on a northeasterly
course. You continue the descent until you cross a
small brook, where you turn sharply right. Here the
trail begins to arc in a half circle before straightening
out to head in a northeasterly direction. The descent
now becomes more pronounced. Through the trees
ahead you will see signs of a single-lane dirt road, on
which you emerge a few minutes later.

Callan Creek, which is one of the headwaters of the
West Branch of the Tioughnioga River, begins at the

top of Hewitt Hill and flows southeast beside the dirt
road on which you are now standing. In 1½ miles it
reaches Cold Brook, which in turn flows into the West
Branch just south of Little York Lake.

Turn left on the dirt road and walk north. This part of
the hike is most pleasant, since the road is canopied by
trees, providing a welcome shade on a sunny day. One-
half mile along the way a road turns off to the left.
Actually, this is a short loop which takes you down to
the creek and then back to the road; hence, it is a nice
place to stop for a break.

When you have rested, continue northward on the dirt
road for another ½ mile, where you intersect a hard-

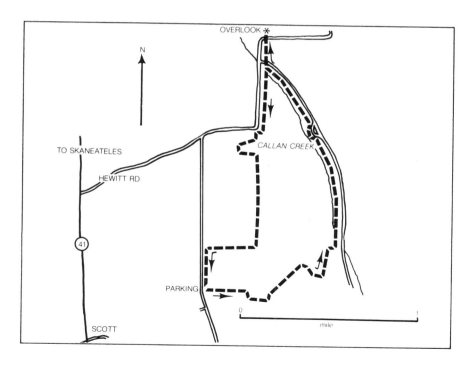

packed, two-lane dirt road. You are back on Hewitt Road. Turn right and walk a short distance to the end of the forest plantation. You are now overlooking open fields; to the northeast you can see Preble Hill and Gifford Hill.

Retrace your steps but continue on the two-lane dirt road for about ¼ mile. Just before it turns sharply to the right a jeep trail enters the forest, straight ahead heading south. Take this trail. After several hundred feet, it turns right and then swings around a gully before again turning south. From this point on the trail runs straight for a little over ½ mile and then turns sharply right. After another five minutes walking, you emerge from the woods onto the road on which your vehicle is parked. Turn left, your vehicle is parked ¼ mile down the road.

During your hike you should have seen many deer tracks on the trail. Hewitt provides good cover, food, and protection to the local deer herd, which can travel south beyond the state land through heavy wood cover west of the hamlet of East Scott. This provides them a sizable range. You also may have noticed raccoon tracks, particularly near the little streams and creeks, for Hewitt State Forest has an abundant supply of small game in addition to its deer herd. If you walk carefully and quietly you may even see some of the wildlife.

Winter activities. This highland area catches the snow from the north, and the forest provides good cover so the snow packs well and stays long. The route described is ideal for Nordic skiing and the trails and roads are wide enough to give the skier adequate room for maneuvering. Hewitt Road is plowed in the winter, giving you direct access to the state forest.

8
Spafford Forest

Hiking distance: 3½ miles
Hiking time: 2 hours
Map: USGS Otisco Valley

Onondaga County, which owns and manages this tract of forest, is not of one mind concerning its official designation. County literature and pamphlets refer to Spafford Forest, but the sign that greets you at the trailhead reads Cold Brook Reforestation Area. Spafford Forest, however, is the more popular name. It consists of a string of five narrow parcels of land running roughly northwest-southeast over the top of a hill eleven miles long. This ridge lies between Otisco Valley to the east and Otisco Lake to the north, and few trails can provide as many overlooks and sweeping vistas as the one you find here.

There are few visitors to Spafford Forest. While the deer season does bring in some hunters, it is rare to meet anyone here at other times. One of the reasons for this neglect is that the county doesn't provide any detailed maps or information about the forest's location, so it is a little difficult to find. It is also some-what out of the way for the urban-based weekend walker, being about thirty-five miles from Syracuse and twenty miles from Cortland. However, this may make it even more of a delight to hike, for nobody is stepping on your heels as you try to enjoy the scenery.

The area is restricted to day-use only; this, of course, means no overnight camping is allowed. And, as a sign informs you at the trailhead, the forest is closed to wheeled vehicles.

Access. To reach Spafford Forest, drive to Little York, which is on NY 281 north of Homer. From Little York, drive south on NY 281 for .6 mile to Pratt Corners and turn right onto Cold Brook Road. You are now 7.5 miles from the trailhead. Follow Cold Brook Road as far as the third road on the right (they all are dirt). You have to count; although the USGS map calls it Craig Road, there is no sign on the corner. The parking area at the trailhead is .2 mile along this road. (If you come from Skaneateles, take NY 41 south to Spafford. Turn left in the village onto Cold Brook Road and drive south 2 miles to the unmarked Craig Road.)

Trail. After you have parked your vehicle, look for a gated jeep/truck trail entering the forest next to the reforestation area sign and just a short distance from the parking lot. Climb under the barrier and head uphill. The trail soon turns to the right and heads up a steeper grade, where a limestone outcropping has been exposed by vehicular use. If you look closely at the broken pieces or at the flattened rocks on the side, you see that some contain small fossils. These are not collector's items, to be sure, but they introduce you to a little of the area's geological history and early lifeforms.

You are probably looking at the outline of a brachio-pod, a small shell-like creature that swam the ocean when this region was under water during the Devonian age, about 310 million years ago. New York is famous for its Devonian fossils, which include tribolites, chin-oids, coral, mollusks, and graptolites, and its fish fossils, many of which can be found here or nearby.

At the top of the hill, turn right and head down a short, gradual slope through a wooded area, a pleasant place

Broad fire lanes lead through the reforestation project at Spafford

during the summer. You soon come to an abandoned wooden shed off on your left and a trail junction: one fire lane leads straight ahead and a more heavily used one leads to your left. Take the latter past a stand of maples to the top of a little hill that opens out to a field (which is private, not county, land). Here is your first fine overlook to the west; you can see across a swamp, Cold Brook Road, and onto forested Ripley Hill.

Your trail now turns right onto a fire lane that runs north past hardwoods on the left and evergreens on the right. Within 300 yards are two impressive overlooks, both to the west but offering more interesting views than the one previously. About 20 yards from the second a less distinct lane comes in from the left. Follow it a short distance to the forest edge and then to the right as it heads north along an old fence. This section of the walk provides more fine views to the west.

After bearing right you rejoin the main fire lane amidst a stand of aspens. Turn left and continue walking north. You soon reach the top of a slight rise and then descend into an open area. A picturesque maple grove to the left makes a nice spot to take a break. Follow the trail through the maples. About 50 feet beyond you break into a forty-foot-wide right-of-way for a gas pipeline. This cut affords you an overlook to the northeast and southwest.

Retrace your steps through the maple grove and back to the point where the two fire lanes merged. This time stay to the left, on the main lane, and in short order you reach the section you walked earlier. Continue back to the wooden shed.

Now bear left onto the fire lane you ignored earlier. It turns right and heads south for 1 mile to the end of county property. The trail is level and the walk easy. In about ½ mile two tall maples, one on each side of the lane, tower over the more numerous evergreens, like sentinels guarding the trail. Just beyond them a short trail on the right leads to a tree-stand used by deer hunters. It is on the boundary between county and private land, and although you cannot see through the dense growth, pitching down ahead of it the hill drops abruptly 800 feet into the Otisco Valley.

The ridge on which you are walking is like a backbone, falling off steeply on the left and more gradually on the west. Further to the south, near the end of the forest, the ridge widens a bit.

As you approach the forest's southern end, the trail bends a little to the right and loops back along the

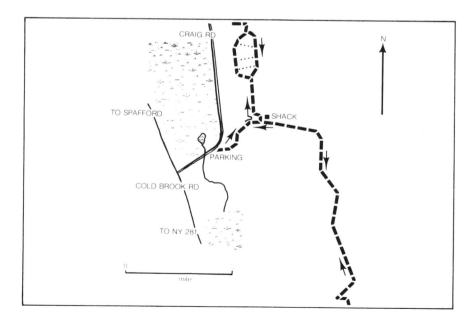

edge of an open crop field. In this section, the woods are more open. It is another fine place for a break. Better still, stretch out on the grass and take a rest —an excellent idea on a warm, sunny day in summer. Over you tower heavy-limbed maples that provide cool shade.

If you look out over the field, you see a tractor/truck road running south for a short distance before bending around the edge of a wood lot. This is private land, but if you stay on the road, you can walk about 100 yards further. From here you can see a small log cabin, which is used during hunting season, at the edge of the woods. Further on where the trees are tallest, is Gifford Hill (el. 1,880') and ¼ mile beyond, Preble Hill (el. 1,880').

Retrace your steps to the junction near the wooden shed and then downward to the road. The walk back is 1¼ miles and should take you no more than thirty or forty minutes.

Winter activities. Here the snow comes early and packs well, providing cross-country skiers with a good base for fast touring. Both skiers and snowshoers should appreciate the varied terrain and winter scenery. The trail system is just long enough to give a nice afternoon workout. Craig Road is plowed to and beyond the parking area, so there is immediate access to the county land.

9
Bear Swamp State Forest

Hiking distance: 8¾ miles
Hiking time: 4½ hours
Maps: USGS Spafford; USGS Sempronius

Bear Swamp State Forest—the name has a forbidding ring to it but fortunately is a little inaccurate. True, there is a forest here—a good-sized one at that—and the state does own a respectable portion of it; however, while there are some narrow wetland stretches and soggy areas, a vast swamp it is not. Nor are there any bears. There may have been a time when the black bear prowled the swamp, but that was before this part of central New York became farming and dairy country. For the last hundred years, bears have not been part of the local landscape.

Once you get past the name and do some hiking in the woods, Bear Swamp may become one of your favorite areas as it has for me. Although the section you will hike consists of only about four square miles of woods, once you enter it you will have a sense of serenity and isolation. The forest itself has an Adirondack-like quality, but the land is relatively flat and the hiking is easy.

What the forest lacks in bears it more than makes up in whitetail deer; in a day's outing you may see three or four of them browsing in the hardwoods, ambling across fire lanes, or leaping with a snort and a flick of their white tails away from the trail for safe cover.

If you are especially careful and observant you may see
one of the wild turkeys that have been stocked here by
the state Department of Environmental Conservation
(DEC) as recently as the winter of 1977. They are wary
creatures, but if you do see one, let the DEC know; it
helps them keep tabs on the survival rate of the birds
they have stocked.

Bear Swamp covers 3,281 acres of high (el. 1,180'), flat
land. On the east side it drops precipitously 800 feet to
the edge of Skaneateles Lake; on the west, however, it
slopes gently downward over a mile's distance to a
narrow swath of brushy wetland through which Bear
Swamp Creek flows.

Access. To reach Bear Swamp State Forest, drive along
the west side of Skaneateles Lake on NY 41A to New

*The bright green leaves of the false hellebore, or Indian Poke,
emerge along brooks and in swamps early in the spring*

Hope. From New Hope continue south on NY 41A for 2.9 miles to Curtin Road, on your left. Follow this two-lane dirt road east to Bear Swamp Road, turn right (south), and drive for .6 mile until you spot a single-lane dirt road on your left. Park your vehicle here on the side of Bear Swamp Road.

Trail. Start your walk by continuing south on Bear Swamp Road. You are now in the thick of the forest, and both sides of the road are lined with large sugar maples that form a canopy during the summer. In a little less than ¼ mile, you intersect Harnett Road.

Turn right on this one-lane dirt road; shortly you reach a bridge over Bear Swamp Creek. The creek is dammed here and a small pond extends back into the thick brush on the south side of the road. The heavy thickets and overgrowth make this swampy portion of the forest nearly impenetrable and, indeed, almost ominous. Luckily, little of the forest is like this; most of it is made up of well-spaced hardwoods and evergreens.

Continue on Harnett Road another ½ mile to a smaller dirt road on the left, which leads south roughly ½ mile through tall stands of evergreens. The road now begins to loop gradually to the left. At the bottom of the loop, you can see through the trees to an open field, and at the end of the loop the trees have changed to hardwood —mostly maples.

Now you are heading north and the road narows to a lane. One-quarter mile ahead you pass a fire lane on your left, and 30 feet beyond, your lane becomes a footpath that is easy to follow. The path turns right and after a couple twists heads north and runs into Harnett Road a short distance from Bear Swamp Creek (which you crossed earlier).

Turn right onto Harnett Road and retrace your steps across the creek to Bear Swamp Road. Now turn right on Bear Swamp Road which too is tree-covered, making it a most pleasant walk, particularly in the summer on a sunny day or in the fall after the leaves have turned.

In about 1 mile the road bends to the right; a short distance beyond, it comes to Ridge Road, on the left. Turn onto this dirt road and continue east for just under ¼ mile until you see a jeep trail bearing off on the left. Turn onto the jeep trail. Your hike for the next mile is along jeep trails. There are three forks; in each case stay to the left to continue north (the right forks form loops with Ridge Road). Near the end of this mile, the jeep trail turns right (east) to intersect Ridge Road. There is an open area here that is used for camping and picnicking, with several cut logs scattered about to use as stools. It is a nice place to take a break.

Turn right on Ridge Road, a hard-packed, single-lane dirt road, and walk south. An old abandoned road runs parallel to it on your right. If you walk this old road, you will find it a bit more scenic. There are spots where weeds have overgrown the roadway and others where the road disappears, but for the most part this "inside" road makes an excellent hiking trail.

In just under a mile you pass a small cemetery on your right, partially enclosed with a white picket fence. As the headstones tell you, it is a family plot for two generations of Wilcoxes. There are six graves here; the first to be buried was Stanton Wilcox, 55, who died in 1855; the last was Lydia Wilcox, 55, who died in 1873. With few words and fewer details we are given a sparse history of a family that homesteaded this land in the nineteenth century and a reminder that even earlier this area had been lumbered and cleared for crop land. It is only as state land that it has been allowed to revert to forest, allowing us to sense what it was like before the settlers came.

About 300 feet beyond the cemetery the road begins a gentle curve to the right. At the bend a jeep trail angles off to the left. Take the jeep trail, which follows the contour of the hill that pitches downward to the east and south reaching Bear Swamp Road in just over ½ mile. The several trails branching off to the right lead more quickly back to Ridge Road. Stay on the main (east-west) jeep trail. This is a most attractive area and a most pleasant walk.

At Bear Swamp Road, turn right (north). A short walk brings you to the corner of Ridge Road where you turned earlier. You can now retrace your steps 1-1/3 miles along Bear Swamp Road to your vehicle.

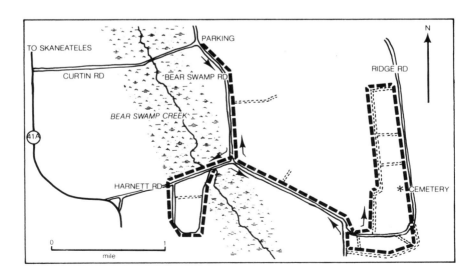

Winter activities. The forest lies within the snowbelt; so the snowfall during January and February is impressive. One cross-country ski shop in Skaneateles conducts ski tours in the forest (which holds the snow well until early spring) using the unplowed roads, jeep trails, and fire lanes as trails. There are enough small hills and bumps to make ski touring interesting, even though ski tourers may have to share the roads with snowmobilers. For snowshoers, networks of jeep trails and footpaths cover a good section of the forest, and the more adventuresome can always try bushwhacking from one road to another.

10
Summer Hill and Fillmore Glen

Hiking distance: 8 miles
Hiking time: 4½ hours
Maps: USGS Sempronius; USGS Moravia

Perhaps it was a place like Summer Hill State Forest that moved the poet Winston O. Abbott to write the invitation: "Come climb my hill and share with me/The quietude of woodlands paths/. . . Evening skies splashed with crimson fires of sunset/. . . Come share these things of beauty." Indeed, the things of beauty are many here, and the hill is not difficult to climb. Combine Summer Hill with its neighbor, Fillmore Glen State Park—a deep, tree-greened cleft in Summer Hill's western slope—and you have a piece of earth where you can feel what one naturalist called "the land's heartbeat."

The name of the state forest is a good clue to its delights, for the best time to hike its trails is during the early summer when the fields and trees have turned a deep green, the air is warm, and the sky is a clean, clear blue. It is then that Summer Hill, like the flowering dogwood blossoms you encounter along your way, is at its peak.

Although the state forest land has a checkerboard appearance on the map, it is large (4,345 acres) and completely forested, primarily with evergreens. It sits atop a set of gentle hills that blend to form a plateau with an average elevation of 1,600 feet. To the west the land pitches sharply down to the towns of Locke and

Moravia, which sit in a narrow, glacial valley, while to the east it slopes more gently down to the hamlet of Dresserville.

The eight-mile loop recommended here allows you to take in the sights and sounds of both Summer Hill State Forest and Fillmore Glen State Park. It starts you in the cool green of Summer Hill's woodlands and then takes you down along the southern rim of Fillmore Glen to its western end, back up the ravine trail past a small but beautiful lake, along the top of Summer Hill with its expansive western vista, and back through stately evergreens to your starting point.

Heading past the site of Millard Fillmore's birthplace

On this hike you can also mix a little history with your walking. The name Fillmore pops up often in this area; it honors Millard Fillmore, the man who became America's thirteenth president after Zachary Taylor died in office in 1850. Although Fillmore was never a man of great renown, he was a New Yorker, and the state has not forgotten its native son. The site of his birthplace, just outside state forest lands, can be reached by Fillmore Road, and a replica of the cabin in which he was born is found at the entrance to Fillmore Glen State Park.

Here you can also see evidence of events that occurred much much earlier. During the Pleistocene epoch continental glaciers invaded New York state, leaving their imprint in the Finger Lakes area with a variety of landforms. These include the rounded, worn-down hilltops, flattened uplands, deeply grooved valleys, and the small, rounded, and sometimes elongated hills called eskers or kames, formed by gravel and sand deposits from glacial streams or from debris that fell into openings in the retreating or stagnant ice.

Another landform, shaped by water erosion in the post-glacial period, can be seen in the many rock gorges and ravines found throughout the Finger Lakes Region. One such gorge is found in Fillmore Glen State Park; into it a tributary stream plunges 800 feet from the top of the Summer Hill tableland down the steeply pitched slopes to Owasco Lake. During the post-glacial period, waters have eaten through the underlying shale and sandstone to form a winding chasm with spectacular cascades, chutes, and falls. As you walk, evidence of glaciation and post-glacial erosion is all around you, giving the area its unique mixture of gentle and rugged landscape.

Access. Summer Hill can be reached easily from
Moravia, about 5 miles south of Owasco Lake. In
Moravia, take NY 38 south to NY 90 in the village of
Locke. Turn left on NY 90 and drive east for 4.4 miles to
Lick Street, a dirt road on the left. Turn here and drive
north for 1.5 miles to the first intersection. Turn left
here onto another dirt road (this is Hoag Avenue,
which becomes Erron Hill Road at the next crossroad;
however, there is no sign at this corner). Drive west 1.1
miles to where Hoag Avenue intersects a north-south
jeep trail. Park your vehicle here.

Trail. You are now in the midst of Summer Hill State
Forest. Start your hike by walking north on the jeep
trail. Shortly you come to a clearing on the right in a
stand of hardwoods, mostly maples. For those
planning a weekend of hiking here, this might be
a good spot to set up camp.

Beyond this point the road gets narrower and less
used. Within ¼ mile you will notice that the ground
becomes wet and boggy; this is a drainage area which
feeds the brook flowing into Fillmore Glen. Within the
next ¼ mile the jeep trail gives way to a single lane that
leads down a short slope to a narrow footbridge
across the brook. Along this trail small orange or yellow
plastic markers are nailed to trees, telling you that this
is a snowmobile trail in the wintertime.

Once you reach the footbridge, retrace your steps
uphill for about 50 yards. Look for a small trail on your
right (west). This is actually a deer trail and it is hard
to find when the weeds begin to grow tall. At this point,
whether or not you find the trail, climb the embankment through the trees to the top. Here an abandoned
road runs parallel to the one you took to the footbridge.
Though it is leaf-strewn and weed-covered, this road
is easy to find.

Turn right onto the abandoned road and follow it as it runs north a short distance, and then west as it follows the contour of the gully on your right. You are now bushwhacking your way along the gully and along the southern edge of Fillmore Glen State Park. In about 100 yards the abandoned road reaches a point where the forest opens up into fields to the east; this marks the end of Summer Hill State Forest and the beginning of Fillmore Glen State Park.

Using the fields as a guide, it is an easy matter to walk the forest edge for the next ¾ mile. You cross two gullies before you intercept a dirt road that bends off to the south and west. Running north from this bend is a snowmobile trail that you may wish to follow down to Fillmore Glen Brook.

Follow the dirt road west for ½ mile, until you reach another road forking to the right. Across this road is a large log, acting as a barrier to all motorized vehicles. Follow this road, which leads in a little over ¼ mile to a paved road. To your right a footpath takes you along the southern rim of Fillmore Glen, which has now turned to a deep ravine on your right.

Follow the path westward until it descends to a picnic area near the park entrance. From the picnic area you can walk upstream a short distance to view the high falls. On your return from the falls, look for a sign directing you up some stone stairs to the gorge trail. This trail takes you past the top of the falls and then along the edge of the stream in the gorge. It is a delightful walk, and the scenery in the gorge is most impressive.

The trail snakes back and forth over footbridges across the stream and then passes a wide, three-story-high waterfall cascading down the north side of the gorge. About 1 mile from the picnic area, the trail crosses to

the north side of the stream bringing you to a small
lake—actually a man-made impoundment designed to
control the water flow through the glen. Follow the
footpath around the dam end of the lake, uphill to your
right, and onto the paved road you reached earlier. You
can now retrace your steps back to the dirt road
walked before and to the bend you intercepted when
bushwhacking. Turn south at the bend and follow the
dirt road as it rises slightly, giving you a fine view to
the west as it passes through open fields.

The road now enters Summer Hill State Forest,
passing through a stand of evergreens. One-quarter
mile takes you through the neck of this section of
forest to Erron Hill Road. Before reaching the road,
however, you have an excellent view of the open land as
it slopes downward to Owasco Inlet Valley. Thickly
forested Jewett Hill rises on the other side.

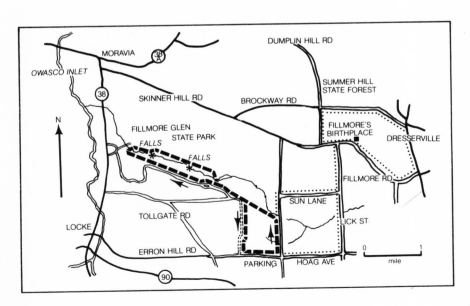

Turn left (east) on Erron Hill Road for the ¾-mile walk through tall evergreens back to your vehicle.

If you are planning a weekend outing in Summer Hill, there are other loops you can walk. One follows the jeep trail you took earlier across Fillmore Glen Brook, then up Sun Lane to Lick Street and back. Still another turns north on Lick Street, runs to Fillmore Road, and then turns north on Dumplin Hill Road to Brockway Road. From here you can walk to Salt Road, which runs south out of Dresserville and back to Fillmore Road, which takes you past the birthplace of Millard Fillmore.

Winter activities. This is not the best area for cross-country skiing. Besides being too flat, most of the dirt roads in the forest are plowed and snowmobilers make extensive use of the few that are not.

11

Chimney Bluff and East Bay Marsh

Hiking distance: 2½ miles
Hiking time: 1½ hours
Map: USGS Sodus Point

Here's a place that delights the eye with the natural wonder of bluff sculpturing—the breath-taking sights of the "chimneys." It is a place where you can hike a Lake Ontario beach and the edge of a 400-foot-high bluff. It also is a place that invites you to engage in a host of enjoyable activities: a picnic on the beach, a swim in Lake Ontario, a canoe trip in the large bay and its four feeder streams, or a hike around the point.

It is called the East Bay Marsh Unit, and for a small parcel of public land, it has much to offer. When the state acquired the land over a decade ago, it was earmarked as a site for a state park. Plans changed and the land remains undeveloped. The thinking now is to preserve it as a "natural" area, a management policy that prohibits the intrusion of housing, toll booths, picnic tables, and other conventional park conveniences. Consequently, it remains attractive and unspoiled.

Access. Chimney Bluff and East Bay Marsh are on Lake Ontario, due north of Seneca and Cayuga lakes and about 2½ miles east of Sodus Bay. From the junction of NY 104, an east-west highway roughly parallel to Lake Ontario's shoreline, and NY 414, which runs north from exit 41 of I-90, turn north on the road to the village of Huron, and then continue north for

On the beach at Chimney Bluff

another 2.5 miles to the hamlet of North Huron, where you turn left. Drive another mile, crossing a stream, and turn right on the paved road that you intersect. In a short distance you cross a bridge, and then the road forks. Bear to your right and continue on this paved road for 1 mile to the beach. Here you will find room on your right to park your vehicle.

Trail. Once you have parked your car, you are at the base of Chimney Bluff, which towers upward abruptly on your left. The face of the bluff drops sharply to within twenty or thirty feet of the water's edge. Start your walk on the pebble-packed beach, heading left (west) as you face Lake Ontario.

Within a few hundred feet you get your first glimpse of the "chimneys"—a series of pinnacles, spires, peaks, saddles, and knifelike ledges that rise 400 feet above the water's edge. These landforms have been etched, eroded, molded, and shaped by constant exposure to wind and water and by the icy spray and wet snow that sweep across Lake Ontario with gale force each winter.

The bluff, a mixture of relatively hard and soft soils, was formed centuries ago by the continental glacier. The surface facing the lake is exposed earth. Here you see the effects of weathering and the work of erosion agents, which remove the soft, soluble soil and rock, leaving behind the more resistant strata in the forms of pinnacles, spires, and hogbacks.

With every step you take along the beach, the scene changes dramatically as new chimneys come into view or your angle of perspective shifts. The bluff towers over you for about ½ mile before tapering off into flat land, which edges the lake for another ½ mile. At this 1-mile point you can look back and view the bluff within the context of the whole coastline.

Now, leave the beach and climb the bank to a footpath. Turn left onto the path and head in the direction of your vehicle. You soon reach the top of the bluff. Here, with every twist and turn off the bluff's edge and along the narrow projections of the hogbacks, the view seems ever more breath-taking. The contrast of the red-brown pinnacles against the blue-green water of the lake is most striking, especially on bright, sunny days.

Be sure to stop from time to time and drink deeply of all this. However, in the midst of this grandeur, don't neglect the simpler beauties that crowd around your feet. Take time, especially in late spring, to observe the vast array of wildflowers that fill the woods crowning the bluff. Sprinkled throughout are the typical forest flowers: phlox, yellow wood-sorrel, buttercup, coltsfoot, mandrake, mitterwort, foamflower, and violets. But most striking is the profusion of painted trilliums, solomon's seals, and columbines. Columbine is found on both sides of the footpath for nearly its entire dis-

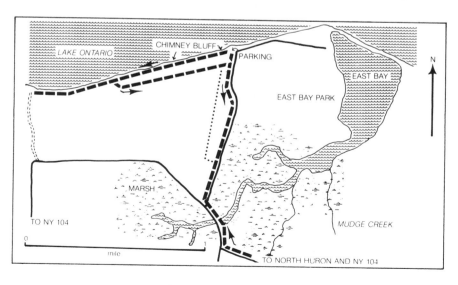

tance. So, too, is a variety of ferns, including large patches of sensitive fern, woodfern, and cinnamon fern.

You finally reach the eastern edge of the bluff, where the path descends to the parking area. It is a short but steep descent, and care is advised.

At this point you can call it a day or continue your exploratory hike. If you are in a hiking mood, head south on the paved road (the one by which you entered), to either of the two bridges you crossed previously. As you come to the first bridge you are over-looking a vast marsh area—a breeding ground for many of the wetland-loving birds, especially ducks. You can see the ducks moving about the marsh almost any time of day, particularly in late spring.

The marsh also makes for fine canoeing. A thin land barrier separates East Bay from Lake Ontario, and four marsh-draining streams feed the naturally impounded bay. If you wish, you can spend a day canoeing these waters. Indeed, it may take you all day, since you will be covering more than 10 miles of water as you canoe up and back each of the four feeder streams.

When either you or the offerings of East Bay are exhausted, retrace your steps to the beach edge and your vehicle.

Winter activities. The area south of the bluff is a bit too flat to offer good cross-country skiing, but it is fine for snowshoeing, and there is much in the marsh that you can explore after the water has frozen solidly enough to permit crossing. The snow may be a little sparse in this area of New York, and you should be prepared for cold, harsh winds coming off the lake. Nonetheless, the paved roads are plowed in the winter, making this area easily accessible.

12
Red Creek Marsh and Scotts Bluff

Hiking distance: 2½ miles
Hiking time: 2 hours
Map: USGS North Wolcott

The Red Creek Marsh Unit, a state-owned parcel of wetland and woods fronting on Lake Ontario, encompasses a variety of natural wonders within its two square miles, among them Scotts Bluff and naturally impounded Red Creek. The creek is ideal for flatwater canoeing and, if you like, even canoe camping along its upper reaches. The different habitats the tract encloses allow you to observe an array of both woodland and shore birds, so, beginner or expert, bring your field guide—you will find many opportunities to use it during your two hours or less of easy walking around this loop.

Access. Your walk begins by Scotts Bluff, 7.6 road miles from Wolcott. Drive east out of Wolcott, toward NY 104, en route to the town of Red Creek. At 2.6 miles you cross Wadsworth Road. Another .8 mile brings you to Hapeman Road, where you turn left and travel 2 miles to an intersection. Turn right, drive .2 mile into the hamlet of North Wolcott, and turn left onto Broadway. In .6 mile you cross Younglove Road, 1,000 feet beyond which is a sign marking the boundary of the Red Creek Marsh Unit.

Another .5 mile brings you to a bridge across Red Creek; on weekends it is often lined with fishermen. All around you are wetlands where, from early spring until late fall, waterfowl nest, feed, and rest. About .9 mile beyond the bridge the road, which turns to dirt after .4 mile, comes to a dead end. You are now on top of Scotts Bluff. Park your vehicle in the small parking area on the west side of the road.

Tall willows line the beach between bluffs

Trail. At the road's end a footpath bending slightly to the right leads to the edge of Scotts Bluff. Here, one-hundred feet above the water, by a process similar to the one that produced the edges, pinnacles, peaks, and "chimneys" of Chimney Bluff (see Walk 11), winds, rains, and spray driven across Lake Ontario and against the relatively soft earth of the cliff face have etched their marks in the form of peaks and saddles to produce this unusual landform.

Return to your vehicle. Facing west you overlook a hay field that slopes down toward the marsh in the southwest and toward Lake Ontario in the northwest. Walk downhill to the steep trail that descends to the beach. Here an endless assortment of brightly colored pebbles and flat rocks cobble the lakeshore. Most of the stones are of a bright reddish hue, and the designs on their smooth, worn surfaces are appealing. You may be tempted to fill your pockets with the most attractive ones—until you remember that you still have a hike to walk.

Back from the water's edge, tall, stately willows line the beach for ½ mile west to the next bluff. Amidst the willows, sand and dirt combine to form a natural path parallel to the lakeshore. Here you see, situated just south of the willow trees, what looks like a pond about ½ mile in length and 500 feet across. This is the east leg of naturally impounded Red Creek. When heavy waves sweep across Lake Ontario during storms, they roll up tons of rocks, stones, and pebbles to form a breakwater several feet high. This breakwater then acts like a dam, preventing the water in Red Creek from emptying into the lake.

Walk west along the natural path until, at the ¼-mile point, a jeep track angles off to the left. Follow this trail

through a wooded area along the edge of the marsh.
You are now heading south on a fingerlike spit of land.
In ½ mile the trail turns to your right, heading over
some high ground and then through a small stretch of
marsh. In just over 100 yards you come to a dirt road.
Turn right and walk north, back toward Lake Ontario.
This is a most pleasant place to pass through,
particularly on a sunny morning when the birds are
most active. The road is completely canopied by trees,
mostly white oaks and maples, and there is always a
cool breeze coming off the lake. Cedar waxwings,
vireos, scarlet tanagers, and towhees are among the
many species you might see or hear. Spring through
autumn this wood is a noisy place, filled with the calls
and songs of the feathered inhabitants.

Another ½ mile brings you to the road's end, at the
edge of a ninety-foot bluff, where you have an excellent

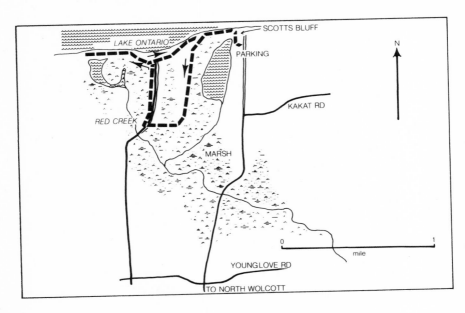

view of the shoreline. To the left a footpath leads for several hundred feet into a wooded area, skirting a small clearing often used by campers. Then it bends right toward the bluff edge and slopes down, passing two summer cottages that occupy a small tract of private land, to the beach.

Once on the beach, continue westward another ¼ mile. Again you find willows lining the upper shore. To the left a narrow neck of water, part of the west leg of Red Creek, comes almost to the beach. Here you can see the interaction of water, land, wind, and waves changing the landscape almost before your eyes: one day the water may be held back by the piled-up pebbles; the next the waves may have washed some of them away, allowing the impounded waters of Red Creek to spill through the small breach into the lake.

Retrace your steps along the beach, up the path, and back to the road at the dead-end turnaround on the ninety-foot-high bluff. Cross the road and walk down the field between the bluff edge and the wooded area on your right. Near the bottom a path leads through a stand of trees and back to the beach. Continue walking east for about 1,000 feet, until you see, on your right, the jeep track you walked earlier. Take the path under the willows to the base of the bluff and go up the footpath to your vehicle.

Winter activities. While this is not ideal terrain for ski touring, being too flat in the marsh area and too hilly near the bluff, snowshoeing the frozen course of Red Creek makes a good outing. Snow conditions range from fair to good during January and February, and the paved roads are plowed regularly, giving you direct access to the state land.

13
Montezuma Refuge

Hiking distance: 8 miles (total)
Hiking time: 4 hours
Maps: USGS Cayuga; USGS Savannah;
*   USGS Seneca Falls*

It is only a pinpoint on most maps, but each fall and
spring it is a stop-over for hundreds of thousands of
Canada geese and an even larger number of ducks and
shore birds of every variety. At the height of the
migration periods, Montezuma National Wildlife
Refuge draws in waterfowl the way a large magnet
pulls in metal filings. In late afternoon, you can watch
long skeins of geese flying into the refuge from every
point of the compass. It is an impressive sight.

The 6,433-acre refuge is located at the north end of
Cayuga Lake in the heart of the Finger Lakes Region.
A wildlife habitat of open marsh, swamp woodland,
and small sections of upland woods and fields, it is
home—or at least a way-station—for an impressive
number of birds, mammals, and fish.

At the last report, 235 species of birds and 48 species
of mammals had been identified in the refuge. The
latter category includes everything from the pygmy
shrew to the whitetail deer, and along with such
common animals as the opossum, woodchuck, snowshoe rabbit, raccoon, fox, porcupine, beaver and
muskrat, there have been reported sightings of the
southern bog lemming, mink, coyote, and even the
bobcat. There are several fishing sites on the refuge
where you may try your luck with brown bullheads,
northern pike, walleye pike, and the hard-to-catch carp.

This, indeed, is the place to bring binoculars, camera, and field guide. Two observation towers overlook the marshes and ponds, providing excellent opportunities for viewing the birds. There are also more than nine miles of dike roads running next to the holding pools, affording the camera buff spots for close-up shots.

Montezuma's marshes are feeding grounds for thousands of waterfowl each year

Eagle "hacking" also takes place in the refuge. Hacking refers to the hand-rearing of young eagles by man. When the eagles become self-sufficient feeders and fliers, they are banded and released by the wildlife biologists. Ten young eagles have been hacked and released since the program was introduced in 1976 by the state Department of Environmental Conservation in cooperation with the U.S. Fish and Wildlife Service and Cornell University. The hacking tree or tower is located at the northern end of Tschache Pool and can be seen from the observation tower at the pool's southern end or from the Clark Ridge Overlook on the west side.

Although waterfowl are present here throughout spring, summer, and fall, the big Montezuma show occurs during the spring and fall migrations, when population peaks reach 70,000 geese and 100,000 ducks. Hundreds of Canada geese funnel into the refuge in late afternoon to various feeding areas. In the morning, geese rarely get themselves airborne much before nine or ten o'clock but the ducks—mallards, blacks, canvasbacks, redheads, teals, pintails, and scaups, to mention the more common varieties—are early risers; they literally fill the morning skies at the crack of dawn.

Access. This waterfowl mecca is located about 20 miles west of Syracuse and 14 miles east of Geneva. It can be reached easily from US 20/NY 5, which passes south of the refuge. A sign points to the refuge entrance on the north side of the highway just west of the Cayuga-Seneca Canal and the junction with NY 90.

The entrance road takes you past the refuge headquarters to a picnic area where there is an information booth. Stop here to pick up maps and pamphlets. (You can also obtain these ahead of your visit by writing: Manager, Montezuma National Wildlife Refuge, RD 1, Box 232, Seneca Falls, NY 13148.) On the northern edge of the picnic area an observation tower gives you a good view of the Main Pool.

Trail. The refuge offers several excellent hiking trails: two are fairly long and four are shorter. The problem is what to select. Not all these trails are connected with footpaths; hence, the starting points of several are best reached by vehicle. On the accompanying sketch map, all the refuge's hiking trails have been designated by letters to facilitate their identification.

The three routes recommended here are the May's Point Pool trail ("M"), the Tschache Pool trail ("T"), and the Esker Brook trail ("E"). To get to the starting point of your hike, drive north 5 miles from the picnic area on the dirt road ("R" trail) flanking the Main Pool. A number of overlooks along this road allow you to view the resting or feeding waterfowl in the pool or the large carp at the outlet during the spawning period. When you reach NY 89 turn right and drive to the Tschache Pool observation tower, just beyond the New York Thruway (I-90) overpass. On your right, you will see the dike road ("M" trail) along the northern edge of May's Point Pool. Start here.

This path is open to the public only from October 1 to March 1; which fortunately allows you to visit during the peak of the fowl migration. The trail runs just to the tip of the pool, making a relatively short walk of 1½ miles that brings you near the feeding waterfowl. When you arrive at the end, retrace your steps to the parking area. You are now ready to begin your walk on the Tschache Pool ("T") trail, which also leaves from here.

This second trail, which runs to the northern tip of the pool is 4¼ miles long. Our walk here is somewhat shorter—only 1¼ miles to the neck of the pool, where the viewing is ideal. On this trail you have an opportunity to get close to the hacking tree, and you may see the young eagles feeding in their nest.

This pool is a favorite of herons. A common sight throughout the summer and early fall is the great blue heron; you may see as many as a half a dozen standing in the water at any one time. June through August is the time for sighting the green heron, which also nests in the refuge. The little blue heron does frequent the area, but is a rare sight.

After returning to the parking area, drive your vehicle south on NY 89 to Kline Road. Turn right and drive north 1.1 miles to the Esker Brook Trail ("E"); a sign on the right tells you when you have arrived at the parking area and trailhead. Your walk here runs about 2¼ miles mostly through hardwoods. A wooden bench halfway around the trail makes a nice place to stop for a rest. It is also an ideal place to observe birds. Wood thrush, vireos, veerys, and warblers are especially abundant here in late May and early June. There are also several overlooks along the trail that allow you good viewing to the east; most of the trail, however, is canopied by trees, providing a cool shade on a warm summer day or a beautiful color display in the fall when the foliage turns.

There are two other hiking trails in the refuge. One is short but attractive, running ½ mile along the southern edge of South Spring Pool. This footpath ("S" trail) is easy to spot from NY 89; a sign points to the entrance.

The Clark Ridge Overlook is the destination of the "C" trail. It is reached by driving north on Kline Road 1.6 miles beyond the Esker Brook Trail parking lot. Park

here. The walk from this point to the overlook is less
than a mile long and is especially pleasant during the
summer and fall. Here you have another view of the
hacking tree.

Winter activities. All the trails mentioned here may be
used for ski touring or snowshoeing. Most are a bit too
flat for good ski touring, although the Esker Brook and
the Clark Ridge Overlook trails are somewhat varied.
The main access roads are plowed, so you can reach
the trails without difficulty.

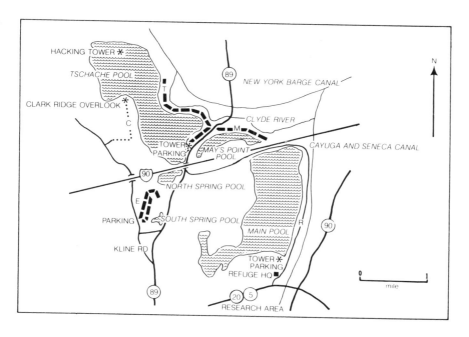

14

Howland Island

Hiking distance: 4 miles
Hiking time: 2¼ hours
Map: USGS Montezuma

The state-owned Howland Island Wildlife Management
Area performs a function similar to that of its close
neighbor, the Montezuma National Wildlife Refuge (see
Walk 13)—namely, to provide a suitable habitat for
waterfowl to rest, feed, and nest. Like Montezuma,
Howland attracts several hundred species of birds,
including a variety of wading and shore birds. During
migratory periods, Canada geese and ducks are the
most numerous visitors, flying into the preserve by the
hundreds.

However, there are several differences between the two
refuges, some of which are important to the hiker. For
one, this 3,600-acre preserve is truly an island. The
Seneca River flows in a huge semicircle around its
northern side, while the southern edge is bounded by
the New York State Barge Canal, which, several
decades ago, acted as the water route to the old Erie
Canal. Because these waterways merge into one
another, they form an island where you normally
wouldn't expect to find one.

Also unlike Montezuma, the main body of Howland
Island is best described as "upland" (a cluster of fields
separated by large stands of hardwood), although it is
surrounded by a strip of marsh wetland along the river
and the canal. The upland section is not heavily

forested; in fact there are several fields planted with
corn to provide food for the wildlife, particularly the
geese and ducks. Interestingly, the ponds used by the
waterfowl are situated in this upland portion not along
the lowland rim. There are also hills on this island—
small ones, to be sure, but hills nonetheless. They add
variety to the landscape and provide hikers with some
fine overlooks.

Still another difference is Howland's large number of
ponds—eleven in all. These are man-made impound-
ments, and most are interconnected. It is primarily in
and around the ponds that a variety of management

Male mallard ducks bob for supper

techniques are employed by the state's Department of Environmental Conservation (DEC) to provide food, cover, and shelter for over 460 species of wildlife.

This is a place to bring your bird guide and field glasses, as well as your camera. Try hiking the island during early or late spring when both land birds and waterfowl are migrating. You may even see several species of hawk, including the sharp-shinned, Cooper, red-tailed, red-shouldered, broad-winged, rough-legged, and marsh hawks. The island is laced with a network of maintenance roads, which are closed to outside vehicles, so you can conveniently reach any part of the island on foot.

There are some periods when hikers are not welcome here; during the waterfowl nesting season in April and May all the refuge except the first mile of main road is closed to the public, and during the October and November hunting season controlled hunting hours prevail. They are usually imposed on Tuesdays, Thursdays, and Saturdays from early morning to noon. For more specific information, call the regional DEC office in Cortland (607-753-3095).

Access. Howland Island is about 8 miles northwest of Cayuga Lake and about 5 miles north of the New York Thruway (I-90). If you come via the Thruway, use exit 40 at Weedsport to pick up NY 31. Drive west on NY 31 to Port Byron and then north on NY 38 for 2 miles to Yellow Schoolhouse Road (.5 mile beyond a set of rail-road tracks). Follow this road to the left. At 1.8 miles, you cross a one-lane steel bridge over the canal. On the far side, to your right, is a public boat-launching site, used extensively by fishermen and canoeists.

You are now on Howland Island. Continue on the two-lane dirt road for another .6 mile to a small green frame building, used during hunting season by the state as a check-in station. Park your vehicle off the road here.

Trail. Your hike begins at the fork in the road about 800 feet north of the building. Bear to your right here and head north. One of the ponds is off on your right, and in the summertime its shoreline is ablaze with the red-flowered fireweed.

Walk around the barrier (which keeps out unauthorized vehicles) and follow the tree-lined road past a small, wooded hill on your left. You are walking along

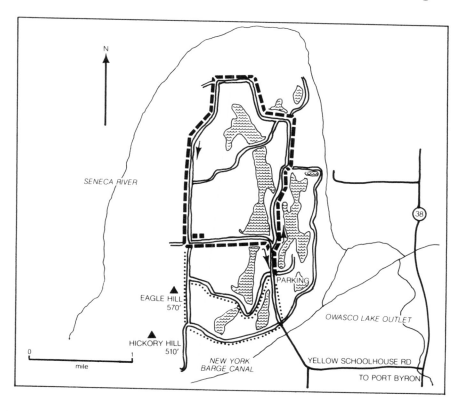

a peninsula, but before you reach its end the road bends to the right across a causeway to another peninsula, where it makes a gradual ascent and then pitches down across a brook. Beyond this brook, another road bears off on your right. Ignore it by keeping left past another wood-covered hill. About ¼ mile beyond it, you come to a T-junction.

Here you are on high ground. Ahead, looking northeast, you can see still another pond, where, as elsewhere in the preserve, you may spot a family of geese during the summer. Turn left at the junction and head downhill (west); this brings you to more water, with the road passing over a causeway at the southern end of the pond.

You now turn north and walk over a small hill to a lowland stretch. In a short distance you may notice some swampland through the trees on your left. Soon the road starts up a gradual rise, passing a right-branching lane as it begins its loop south. You are now walking through a relatively thickly wooded area where trees canopy the road.

Shortly the trees give way to fields on both sides. This is high ground where only small patches of trees obstruct the view. The road bends slightly to the right and then to the left, setting you on a straight southerly course; 1¼ miles more bring you to a cluster of buildings, the Howland Island staff headquarters, and another east-west road.

Turn left here. This road now runs gradually downhill for ¼ mile and then crosses another impoundment. Beyond the causeway, the road turns right (south) and in ⅓ mile returns you to your vehicle.

There are other trails you can follow on the island. One pleasant walk takes you south past the staff headquarters to a fork. If you bear left (the "A" loop on the sketch map) you pass through a heavily wooded area, cross a narrow neck of another impoundment, and eventually return to your vehicle.

To lengthen your walk a bit, you can bear right at the fork and continue south (the "B" loop), past Eagle Hill on your right, across a dam, along the southern edge of still another impoundment, uphill to the main road, and then left along the road back to your vehicle. If you care for a good view of the island, climb the short distance to the top of Eagle Hill, at 570 feet the highest point on the island.

Winter activities. Howland is a fine place for snow-shoeing, but is ideal for ski touring. The terrain, with its small rolling hills, provides a whole series of short downhill runs to add a bit of excitement. Yellow School-house Road is plowed in winter, but you should check with the DEC before attempting the section leading onto the island. The snow conditions on the island are generally good, and in January and February, the snow is plentiful.

15

Tuller Hill
State Forest

Hiking distance: 9½ miles
Hiking time: 5 hours
Maps: USGS McGraw; USGS Cortland

Nice things can come in small packages, as the Tuller
Hill State Forest shows. Here are tall, spaced
hardwoods and tight stands of evergreens, peaked
hilltops and rounded knolls, deep ravines and gentle
glens, rushing brooks and meandering streams, and,
for those who like to see the rugged countryside as well
as feel it, numerous overlooks. Tucked in this cluster of
wooded hills south of Cortland and just west of the
Tioughnioga River are abandoned roads and jeep trails
and a short, relatively new trail that is a delight to hike.

The Tuller Hill Trail, constructed by the Onondaga
Chapter of the Adirondack Mountain Club, will
eventually be joined to other trails to form part of the
state-wide Finger Lakes Trail system (FLT). This
stretch has also been designated part of the North
Country Trail, a route that, while still largely in the
planning stage, will someday wend across the northern
part of the United States from Maine to California. On
this hike, you follow the well-groomed and clearly
blazed (in white) Tuller Hill Trail out, and a series of
dirt roads and trails back.

Access. To reach the trailhead, follow NY 90 west from
NY 11, passing through the hamlet of Messengerville.
At 4 miles watch for Carson Road, which cuts sharply
back and uphill on your right. Follow this road 1.2

miles to the top of the hill, where the forest edge comes
right to the road, and park. The word Hike painted in
white on a tree to your left marks the southern entry to
the Tuller Hill section of the FLT. Before entering the
woods, though, pause long enough to enjoy the
excellent view south overlooking the Gridley Creek
valley. The hills are tree-covered and their sides steep;
the valley is narrow and winding.

Trail. From your vantage point at 1,700 feet above sea
level, you climb another 200 feet over the next ¼ mile
to the level summit of Tut Hill. For the next ¾ mile the
trail runs along the ridge of Tut Hill; it then starts a
gradual descent into Riordan Hollow, crosses Riordan
Brook, and, bearing left, continues its downward
journey another ¾ mile into Woodchuck Hollow. At
1,500 feet, this hollow is the lowest point in the Tuller
Hill Forest.

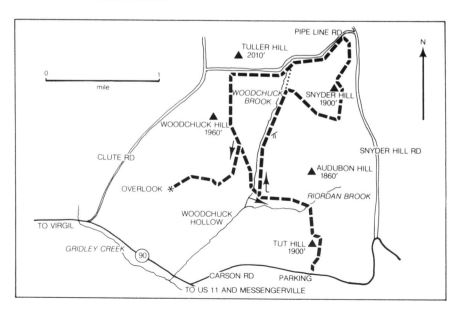

In the hollow, the trail turns north along an abandoned wagon road that parallels Woodchuck Brook, which flows southward through the relatively deep cut between the Tut, Audubon, and Snyder hills on its east and Woodchuck and Tuller hills on its west. The canopy of trees, the wide lane, and the sound of running water make this section of the hike especially attractive—so much so that you scarcely notice the gradual uphill grade. In about ¾ mile, a small clearing and the Woodchuck Hollow lean-to come into view. Those planning an overnight hike should camp here.

Looking westward toward Tuller Hill

As it passes the lean-to the trail leaves the old wagon road. After ½ mile, it brings you to the Neal Brook spur trail, which is blazed with orange markers. Your route, the main trail, follows the white blazes to the right and uphill.

Swinging southeast, you cross a dirt road in ¼ mile and a pipeline right-of-way in another ¼ mile. Here the trail turns north again, following the contour of Snyder Hill. Several overlooks allow you to enjoy the scenery across the Tioughnioga River to the east.

Still following the contours of Snyder Hill, the trail bends left, and you climb almost to its summit (el. 1,900') before bearing right. After a moderate descent for ¼ mile, it intersects a dirt road unimaginatively called Pipe Line Road. In ½ mile you should spot the other entrance to the Neal Brook spur trail by the edge of a small ravine on the left. Remain on Pipe Line Road. In about ¾ mile, watch for a jeep trail leading away from the road on your left. Directly opposite, about 1,000 feet through the stand of hardwoods, you can see the summit of Tuller Hill, at 2,010 feet the highest point in the state forest. To get to its summit you have to bushwhack.

Turn left to follow the jeep trail, which runs relatively level for nearly ¼ mile before heading downhill; here, about 500 feet off to your right, is yet another high point in the forest: Woodchuck Hill. The top of this hill is forested, but the lower sections are not.

Continuing downhill for just over ¼ mile, the trail reaches the state forest's boundary. For a magnificent overlook, stay on the unmarked foot trail as it bends slightly right and flattens out to follow the contour of a hill through stands of saplings and small trees. After ¼

mile, it swings uphill and another ¾ mile brings you to
an open field, where the trail ends. But before you
spreads a grand view of valleys and distant hills.
Immediately below is the Gridley Creek valley, NY 90,
and Virgil Creek valley; directly across are the ski
slopes of Greek Peak on Virgil Mountain (see Walk 16).

After drinking in the view, retrace your steps to the
state forest boundary. If you look off to your right at the
forest edge, you should spot an abandoned road
running gradually downhill. (During the winter, this
old road becomes a snowmobile trail.) Walk down this
track nearly ½ mile to a gully on your left, and then
follow this gully to the base of the hill and Woodchuck
Brook. Cross the stream and climb the embankment
opposite. On top you intersect the main Tuller Hill Trail
you hiked earlier. Turn right and head back 1¾ miles
to your vehicle.

Winter activities. The snow is deep here and it lasts
well into March, providing excellent ski touring and
snowshoeing conditions along the main trail and Pipe
Line Road. Carson Road is plowed, so there is direct
access to the trail.

16
Virgil Mountain

Hiking distance: 4¾ miles
Hiking time: 2 hours
Map: USGS Harford

This is high country, affording you some fine views of peaked and forested hills and narrow, winding valleys without demanding that you scramble up and down on rocky mountain paths. An easy hike, this route combines a loop on dirt country lanes around Kennedy State Forest (named for this district's first state forester) with a short climb up the western slope of Virgil Mountain. While most of the state land is forested, there are large open areas, giving good visibility in all directions.

The highest point on the upland ridge south of Cortland, Virgil Mountain is more popularly known as Greek Peak, after the commercial ski center whose alpine runs dominate the mountain's north slope.

Access. Your starting point for this loop walk is a dirt road on the "back" side of Virgil Mountain. From the intersection of NY 90 and NY 11 south of Cortland, follow NY 90 west, through Messengerville, for 1.5 miles to East Virgil, and then turn left (south) onto Parker Street. After 2.7 miles on this paved road, turn right (west) onto Valentine Hill Road, a dirt road listed on the USGS map as Dann Road. Drive 3 miles and watch for another dirt lane on your left; this is Black Road (there is no sign to identify it). Park here at the intersection.

Maples add brilliant color to a woods walk

Trail. Begin your hike by walking northward on Valentine Hill Road. At nearly the ¼-mile point, as the road bends to the left near a large stand of evergreens, look to the right-hand side for a small sign that reads X-CB. This is a marker for one of the cross-country ski trails maintained by the Greek Peak Ski Center on the unplowed roads of the state forest. Immediately to the right of the sign you should spot a woods road whose entrance has been bulldozed closed to prevent unauthorized vehicles, primarily snowmobiles, from passing.

Turn right and walk down the woods road. In 50 yards you step out of the trees into an open area that pitches sharply downward. You have a fine view of high hills across the deep valley just below. To your right a wide swath has been cut through the trees. This cut is but one of the many downhill ski trails that make up Greek Peak Ski Center.

Bear left, following the road uphill another 150 yards. You are now on top of Virgil Mountain, facing the dismount platform of one of the ski area's chairlifts. Next to the platform a large sign diagrams the various ski slopes.

From here, the view is most spectacular, for you are now at the highest point (el. 2,132') along the ridge that stretches southeast from Cortland toward Marathon. At your feet, the hill drops precipitously 732 feet. Across the narrow valley you can pick out Tuller Hill (see Walk 15) and, to the left, the high rolling hills that extend north beyond the village of Virgil. Continuing on the road beyond the summit another 200 yards, you can reach a second chairlift. Here, too, you are treated to a fine view, this one looking eastwards down the valley toward Messengerville.

Now retrace your steps to Valentine Hill Road, and turn right (north) to continue your walk along the shaded dirt roads of Kennedy State Forest. After ¾ mile, the road tops a rise; to your right open fields allow you a good view to the north and northeast. Ahead, Valentine Hill Road descends sharply and another dirt lane, Stillman Road, bears to the left and uphill.

Your route follows Stillman Road, which leads up between two rows of stately maples and then runs level. After ¾ mile, you come to Courtney Road, where you turn left (south). Another tree-lined dirt lane through open farmland, Courtney Road runs gradually downhill for ¾ mile to Ryan Road. The walk along both Stillman and Courtney roads is most pleasant, especially during the late spring and the fall, when the leaves are changing color. In summer the leafy canopy provides welcome shade on hot days, and throughout the year the open fields on both sides offer attractive views of the surrounding country, including

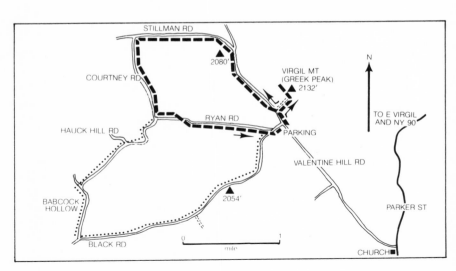

a good one of the tree-covered ridge just south of Virgil Mountain.

At the junction with Ryan Road, you have a choice. If you wish, you can take an alternate and longer loop by continuing south on Courtney Road until you reach Black Road, where you turn left (east) to return to your vehicle. This loop, from Ryan Road back to your vehicle is about 4½ miles long and adds about 2 more hours to your hiking time. It takes you into narrow, wooded Babcock Hollow, through which the headwaters of the East Branch of Owego Creek flows, and then on Black Road through some open areas, giving you a good view of the Harford Hills to the west. Just beyond the halfway mark you will reach a high point (el. 2,054') with a good view north toward Virgil Mountain.

Those who wish to complete the shorter loop should turn onto Ryan Road; from here it is a little over 1 mile back to your vehicle. As you walk east on Ryan Road, you find that it makes a short but gradual descent past a house on the left and then crosses two small brooks. You then begin a gradual climb only to turn downhill again as the road dips to cross another small brook. It then rises gradually until it intersects Black Road. Turn left onto Black Road; a short walk brings you to Valentine Hill Road and your vehicle.

Winter activities. This is great snow country, and the terrain is ideal for cross-country skiing. Most of the dirt roads in the state forest are not plowed in winter, and they make fine trails. Greek Peak Ski Center has laid out marked ski-touring courses in this area. For more information you can call or stop at the Greek Peak Ski Center office on NY 90, about 2½ miles east of the village of Virgil.

17
Yellow Barn
State Forest

Hiking distance: 4½ miles
Hiking time: 2½ hours
Map: USGS Dryden

Yellow Barn State Forest—an odd name, indeed. Whatever else you may see here (and there is much to see), you will not spot any barns, much less a yellow one, for whatever served as the namesake for this area has long since disappeared. What you will find here is a tract of heavily forested hill country just south of Skaneateles Lake—an inviting and delightful locale for the hiker.

This area is particularly attractive during the summer months, with its cool green rolling hills and gentle, grass-covered valleys. It was settled and farmed in the early 1800s, but, like much of the land in this region, it was sold to the state in the 1930s. Today it is public forest land and the domain of the whitetail deer.

Many high points and overlooks add to the appeal of the hike through the forest. On the loop described here, you pass several excellent vistas, and by the time you return to your starting point you will have scanned the rolling landscape south of Cortland, east of Ithaca, west of Marathon, and north of Slaterville Spring. It is an impressive eyeful.

Yellow Barn State Forest has dirt roads, jeep trails, abandoned wagon roads, and bike trails, but it does not have any marked hiking trails. Although there is little danger of becoming lost here, it is a good idea to bring a USGS map and compass in your day pack. The map will help you locate the high spots and give you a better "feel" for the area, the terrain, and the road and trail network.

Access. Yellow Barn State Forest can be reached via NY 13, by driving east from Ithaca or south from Cortland. Coming from Cortland you can see the hills that make up Yellow Barn State Forest as you approach Dryden, where the highway makes a ninety-degree turn and heads west. After crossing Virgil Creek on Dryden's west boundary, drive 1.1 miles to Irish Settlement

Leaving the road to walk across fields open to the sky

Road on the left. Follow it south 1.5 miles to the top of a steep hill. Stop here and park your vehicle on the shoulder by a dirt road that runs off to your right.

Trail. Leave your vehicle and walk west on the dirt road which here passes through private land. On the right, openings through the trees and hedgerows offer you excellent views of the fields and hills spreading north to Cortland. On a clear day you should be able to see fifteen to twenty miles north.

Soon you move into a more forested area, and just past the ½-mile point the road turns ninety degrees left and heads south. Here you will find several jeep trails radiating to the northwest, west, and southwest. Ignore them, and stay on the dirt road.

About 100 feet from the junction you reach the highest point (el. 1,888') in the state forest. This hilltop has no name. Actually you are walking a ridge; so the road is relatively flat and easy to walk.

Continue southward past a power line. A short distance beyond, an abandoned road runs parallel to the main road a few feet to your right. Take it, for it makes an ideal hiking trail.

For the next ¾ mile the trail passes through dense woods before coming to a small clearing on the right through which a logging road passes. Just 100 feet beyond the clearing, the main dirt road turns left, continuing for about 200 more feet before turning right into private property. Do not turn left on the main road, but notice that there is a jeep trail that continues south and another that turns right and heads west. The hike described here follows the right-hand track. (However, if you would like to lengthen your hike, you can include a part of the southern jeep trail which runs along the north-south ridge for about ½ mile to an unnamed high point (el. 1,870') before descending into Sixmile Creek Valley, where Irish Settlement Road circles the southern part of the state forest.)

Turn onto the jeep trail to your right and walk west. Within 200 yards it begins a gradual descent that becomes steeper as you continue. In about ¼ mile the main jeep trail turns to the right and comes to a dead end, while another much less used track bears to the left.

Follow the left-hand road, which continues downhill, eventually crossing a brook. It then heads up a small grade, and, 800 feet beyond, intersects Yellow Barn Hill Road, a single-lane dirt road.

Turn right onto Yellow Barn Hill Road. The road runs due north up a slight incline for almost ½ mile to an area where the hardwood forest opens on your left to reveal a field that sits on higher ground; this is the summit of Yellow Barn Hill. As the high point on the west side of the state forest it has an elevation of 1,840 feet. If you leave the road and make the short climb to the top, you will be treated to a fine view of miles of landscape spreading to the west toward Ithaca.

From this high point it is a short walk (about 100 feet) down the road to a little-used jeep trail that forks to the right. This trail may be somewhat difficult to find, especially during the summer months when the roadside weeds tend to obscure the entrance. (Should you miss the jeep trail, you can continue for another ¼ mile to a power-line crossing and take the truck road underneath it on the right back to your vehicle.)

After making your right turn, you soon find that the trail widens as it moves into a stand of evergreens, making it pleasant to walk. It emerges from the forest in a little less than ½ mile onto the power-line right-of-way, intersecting the truck road mentioned earlier.

Turn right onto the truck road. After walking past two power-line poles, you come to the dirt road you walked earlier. Cross the road and continue on the power-line right-of-way for the next ½ mile. This walk gives you a good view of the two hills that dominate the eastern section of the state forest; the power-line road dips downward sharply at first and then levels out for the next ¼ mile as it passes through some open fields before rising to cross a small hilltop.

From the hilltop you descend 200 feet to the Irish Settlement Road. Cross this paved road and continue

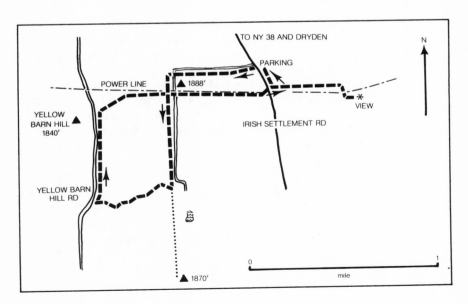

up the dirt road that parallels the power line. Trees line both sides, shading it in the summer. A ¼-mile walk uphill brings you to a road barrier and posted signs. A jeep trail swings off to the right onto state land and then continues to the top of the hill (el. 1,850'). Follow it to have a nice view of the countryside off to the east, including Virgil Creek valley and Dryden Lake.

Retrace your steps to Irish Settlement Road, turn right, and walk little less than ¼ mile back to your vehicle.

Winter activities. These hills receive their share of snow, making this a pleasant area for snowshoeing and cross-country skiing. Irish Settlement Road is plowed in the winter, giving you access to the forest. There is enough variety to make ski touring enjoyable, and if you follow the route suggested above, you should be able to ski the area in about two to three hours.

18
Shindagin Hollow

Hiking distance: 3½ miles
Hiking time: 2 hours
Map: USGS Speedsville

There is a long north-south valley, almost gorgelike in
its narrowness, located ten miles southeast of Ithaca
and Cayuga Lake. Called Shindagin Hollow, it was once
the route of a well-used Indian trail that ran northeast
from the main Cayuga-Owego trail to what is now the
village of Caroline, where it met another heavily
traveled Indian route, the Onondaga-Owego trail.
Today this valley sits in the heart of a large parcel of
state land which, appropriately, bears its name:
Shindagin Hollow State Forest.

Running in an east-west direction through the forest
and across the hollow is the well-marked Caroline
section of the main Finger Lakes Trail (FLT),
maintained by the Cayuga Trails Club. The trail
markers are white blazes. By using portions of this
trail and taking advantage of the network of dirt roads
that lace the state forest and adjoining lands, it is
possible to devise several delightful loops that will take
you through wildernesslike stretches of forest, into
deep ravines and narrow valleys, and over open high
spots where you can see miles of the surrounding
countryside. The entire area is situated on a high
tableland averaging about 1,500 feet above sea level.
The scenic variety found in the forest makes this one
of the most attractive sections of the FLT.

The hiking loop recommended here is relatively
short (3½ miles), but it gives you a good sample of the
region's charm, covering some open highland
with views to the north and east, a part of the narrow Shindagin Hollow, and a deep ravine that the
FLT follows along its eastern rim to the Shindagin
Hollow lean-to.

The lean-to is a good place to spend the night if you
would like to cover more territory and explore other
sections of the FLT. From the starting point for this
hike the FLT continues eastward through another
parcel of state land with the rather pedestrian name of
Potato Hill State Forest. Continuing northward you
arrive at the region's highest point at Padlock Lookout
Tower (el. 1,900'), from which you can see twenty to

*Scaly polypore, a fungi that typically appears in the same place
year after year*

thirty miles in all directions. You can also follow the
FLT to the west out of Shindagin Hollow, across
Willseyville Creek in the adjoining valley, and into
another unusually attractive region where you will
enter Danby State Forest (see Walk 19).

Whatever your preference, you are walking in one of
the most heavily forested areas in central New York.
With its rolling hills and lush valleys, it is a delight to
the eye and a boon for the hiker.

Access. To reach the trailhead from Ithaca, drive east
on NY 79 for 5 miles to NY 330, which forks to your
right. Continue on NY 330 another 5 miles until you
intersect Old Seventysix Road at the junction called
Guide Board Corners. Turn right onto this road and
drive 2.4 miles to the hamlet of Caroline Center.

If you are approaching from I-81, exit at Whitney Point,
and follow NY 79 west 21 miles. Look for Old Seventysix Road on your left just beyond the village of Slaterville Springs; once on Old Seventysix Road, drive to
Caroline Center.

In Caroline Center, turn south onto South Road, a
two-lane hard-packed dirt road. Drive 1.2 miles to
Gulf Creek Road, on your right. Park your vehicle at
the intersection.

Trail. Start your hike by walking west on Gulf Creek
Road, which runs through open fields giving you a
good view of the countryside to the north and west. For
the next ½ mile the road descends gradually, crossing
a trickle of a brook (in spring), and then begins a short
ascent to the forest edge. You are now entering the
northern section of Shindagin Hollow State Forest at
one of the high spots of the region (el. 1,550').

A short distance into the forest the road turns sharply left and heads south. Within several hundred feet it begins the descent into Shindagin Hollow. It is a 1-mile walk from the road's turn to the bottom of the hollow; about halfway down the road pitches downward more sharply, and the slope becomes more pronounced as you near the bottom. The trees along the road provide cool shade during the summer.

At the bottom, Gulf Creek Road intersects Shindagin Hollow Road. You are now in a narrow ravine with forested sides that rise sharply almost 350 feet. Flowing through the hollow is Shindagin Hollow Creek.

Turn left onto Shindagin Hollow Road and follow it south for about 100 feet. To your left you will see a cut into the side of the hill. It is the outlet of a deep, narrow gorge; the FLT follows its eastern rim. During the early spring as the snow waters roar down the mile-long gorge, you are treated to an impressive sight here. At the outlet, just before the spot where the waters pour into the Shindagin Hollow Creek, there is a narrow cut in the shale rock. As the waters rush through this cut each spring, they form a raging cataract. Shindagin is a corruption of the word Shandaken, an Indian word meaning "rapid water." It was probably here during the spring run-offs that the Indians watched the torrential waters of the gorge meeting these of Shindagin Hollow Creek and spoke of the place as Shandaken.

A few feet south of this point on Shindagin Hollow Road, a white FLT marker directs you across the creek (during the summer and fall it is a dry stream bed) to an abandoned road. Follow this road uphill. The initial climb of several hundred feet is quite steep, but soon the road levels out. After a gentle ½-mile climb, the trail

turns sharply to your left and begins a gradual downward pitch. Within a short distance the trail flattens.

To your left is a thirty-foot drop into a ravine; ahead
and little to your right is the Shindagin Hollow lean-to.
The hemlocks surrounding it make this a most
inviting place to stop for a break or to stay overnight.

Follow the white blazes of the FLT as they take you
north past the lean-to. The trail snakes through the
forest along the ravine's edge for about ¼ mile, and
then it turns right taking you up for ½ mile on a
straight easterly course to South Road. Once on South
Road, turn north. In less than ½ mile, you are back
with your vehicle.

The FLT crosses South Road, and, if you like, you can
add a few more miles to your hike by continuing

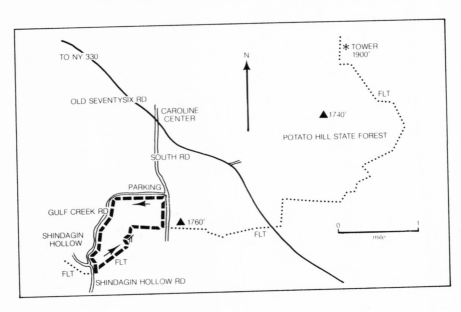

eastward. The trail takes you through a hardwood forest for 1½ miles and eventually across Boyer Creek to the paved highway, Old Seventysix Road. If you stay on the FLT, another mile brings you to the Potato Hill State Forest; the walk through this forest is 2¼ miles long and another mile to the north brings you to the Padlock lookout tower.

Another loop that you may wish to add to the recommended hike follows Shindagin Hollow Road north for 1 mile. Here a jeep trail forks to the left and runs south, almost paralleling Shindagin Hollow Road. If you follow this jeep trail, you will intersect the east-west FLT. You can then turn left (east) on the FLT and follow it downhill to the hollow and back onto Shindagin Hollow Road.

Winter activities. These hills hold the snow well. Most of the dirt roads in the area are plowed, giving you direct access to the FLT. This section is ideal for cross-country ski enthusiasts as the terrain is just varied enough to make ski touring challenging and interesting.

19
Danby State Forest

Hiking distance: 9 miles
Hiking time: 4½ hours
Map: USGS Willseyville

Danby State Forest is a large land tract (7,086 acres) situated 14 miles south of Ithaca. It occupies the highland region just south of NY 96B, a highway that runs southeast from Ithaca to Owego, passing through the hamlet of Danby, from which the state forest derives its name. This high area is tableland, a rolling, wooded landscape mixed with open fields. It is uncommonly picturesque, especially in late spring or early summer when the valleys are carpeted in deep green and the hilltops are still dressed in softer, yellow-green.

Essayist and naturalist Hal Borland wrote that "half the benefit, and even more of the satisfaction, of walking comes from the leisurely change of scene." In Danby, there is always a leisurely change of scene. Here you find long fields as well as deep woods, tree-lined lanes as well as meandering foot trails passing through forest glens and sun-washed glades; and with each new turn comes a change in mood. You can literally walk for miles without seeing any houses, farms, or people; and yet this sense of remoteness is complemented by a feeling of openness that results from the many overlooks where the surrounding hilltops and valleys spread out before you.

Danby State Forest is a long swath of land bounded on the west by Michigan Hollow, on the north by Danby

Creek Valley, and on the east by Willseyville Valley. The region has a distinctive geological characteristic in its sharply pointed hilltops with steep sides and narrow valleys, making the landscape look more rugged and mountainous than it actually is. Most of the hills barely rise over 1,600 feet, yet they look much higher.

Through all of this run eight miles of Finger Lakes Trail (FLT), built and currently maintained by the Cayuga Trails Club, one of the several sponsoring groups of the Finger Lakes Trail Conference.

Michigan Hollow got its name from early settlers who started for Michigan but decided to stay here instead, giving the area the name of their once hoped-for destination. Geologically, the hollow straddles a divide, with water flowing out of one pond northward to form Buttermilk Creek, which eventually empties into Cayuga Lake, and out of another nearby pond southward to form Michigan Creek, which flows to the Susquehanna River.

Willseyville Valley and nearby Danby Creek Valley are what geologists call "through valleys," carved by glaciers which deepened the valleys and steepened the hillsides. The east side of Eastman Hill is a good example of such oversteepening, with a drop of 700 feet into Willseyville Valley at about a thirty-five-degree angle.

Willseyville Valley is also known as the "Warrior's Trail." It was the main Indian trail from Cayuga Lake to the Susquehanna River, and the route taken by the Indians and Tories in 1779 during the Revolutionary War to harass troops of the Continental Army which were seeking to join the Sullivan Expedition. The first settlers who came to Ithaca from Owego in 1789 used this trail, widening it for their ox carts.

The hike recommended here begins on South Danby
Road and runs eastward over the highest point of the
region, downhill and across NY 96B, and up to the top
of Eastman Hill. With several substantial climbs it is a
moderate-to-difficult hike, but the effort is worth it.

Access. The trailhead can be reached by taking NY
96B south from Ithaca 6.4 miles to Danby. Continue
through Danby another 2.6 miles to paved South
Danby Road on your right. This road can also be
reached from the south by taking NY 96B; then drive
north through Willseyville for 4.5 miles to South Danby
Road, on your left.

*In Danby you can literally walk for miles without seeing any
houses, farms, or people*

Once on South Danby Road, drive south 1.5 miles and watch for white blazes on both sides of the road, indicating where the FLT crosses. The first blaze is on the right. Drive beyond it over a small brook (Miller Creek) for 225 feet. Another FLT marker can now be seen on your left. Park here.

Trail. Follow the FLT uphill to the east; in several hundred feet you reach an abandoned road that runs due east. The FLT, marked by white blazes, follows this road steadily uphill for almost 1 mile through thick woods, mostly pines and hemlocks. As you near the top of the hill the ascent becomes more moderate, and the trail finally levels out as you pass through a stand of pines just before reaching Travor Road.

Turn left and follow this dirt lane northward for about ¼ mile until it bends to the left. Leave Travor Road and follow the FLT to the right along an old farm road past a cellar hole. Shortly the trail takes you into a stand of larches where it bends to the right, moving through a small clearing, and then turns left (north) into another larch plantation. For the last ¼ mile you have been making a moderate ascent. You now are almost at the highest point (el. 1,758'), in the region; this unnamed hilltop is in the woods just off to your left. A little farther along a spur trail bears off to the right about 100 feet to the Tamarack lean-to, a delightful place to spend the night.

Just beyond the spur trail, the main trail pitches downward. The hill here is quite steep; in less than ¾ mile you descend 584 feet. En route you pass a second spur trail which goes south about 100 feet to a spring. Continue downhill through the woods until you emerge in an open area; turn left for a short distance and continue until you reach a small stream (Danby Creek) at the base of the hill. Just ahead is NY 96B, and across Danby Creek Valley you see a cluster of hilltops: Durfee Hill, Roundtop, and Eastman Hill.

Follow the creek a short distance to a culvert and NY 96B. Cross the highway and pick up the white blazes on the other side. Soon you encounter a fence, which you follow for about 100 feet to enter an open field. Across the field you can see a white blaze painted on a stick. Follow the trail to this point, then cross the rest of the field to the bottom of the hill where the FLT enters the woods and starts uphill on a generally easterly course.

In about ½ mile the trail leaves the woods and crosses a field, skirting a pond on the left and continuing uphill through a small stand of pines. Here the trail swings left and goes north uphill through an abandoned field. You are now at the top of an unnamed hill, having climbed 476 feet from Danby Creek Valley.

The trail crosses a little-used road and passes through a field containing aspen trees. To your right you have a fine view to the southeast. Follow the trail as it dips down into a shallow, wooded valley, passes through pines, and then heads uphill through a stand of locust trees to emerge on Eastman Hill Road, a single dirt lane. Cross the road and continue uphill for about ¼ mile along a hedgerow; then follow an old farm road through a field. You are now on top of Eastman Hill (el. 1,690'). If you continue a few hundred yards in this direction, you should be able to see east through the trees and glimpse Willseyville Valley 595 feet below.

Now retrace your steps to Eastman Hill Road. Turn left (south), and in a short distance you come to Heisy Road, another single dirt lane. Turn right (west), and follow Heisy Road downhill to NY 96B where you turn right and walk ¼ mile north to pick up the FLT.

You can now retrace your route on the FLT uphill past
the lean-to, across Travor Road, and then downhill to
your vehicle.

An alternate route back to your vehicle takes you right
(north) on Travor Road and then west to the intersection with South Danby Road. Turn left (south) here
and walk ¾ mile back to your vehicle. This route takes
you over a hill and through some fields, offering you
delightful views to the north, east, and south.
You may lengthen your hike during a weekend
outing by following the FLT west from the spot
where you parked your vehicle. A 3-mile walk
brings you to Michigan Hollow, where the FLT
crosses Michigan Creek.

Winter activities. If you stay on the tableland and
avoid the steep hills pitching down to NY 96B, this is
a fine area for snowshoeing and ski touring. Snow
conditions are good during January and February,
and South Danby Road (which is plowed) offers easy
access to the FLT.

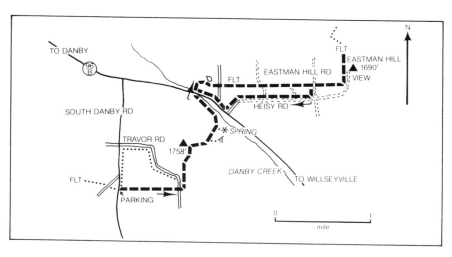

20
Enfield Trail

Hiking distance: 9½ miles
Hiking time: 5 hours
Maps: USGS Mecklenburg; USGS Ithaca West

Call it the Enfield Connection; it is a section of the
Finger Lakes Trail (FLT) that connects two large pieces
of state land: Connecticut Hill State Game Management Area in the west, and Robert H. Tremen State
Park in the east. In between are high spots that give
you fine, wide views of distant ridges—some of them
twenty and thirty miles away. You'll walk in quiet glens
and cool forests, along abandoned wagon roads
meandering through stands of maples, beeches, and
oaks, and over sparkling brooks. Finally, you'll enter a
deep gorge cut by Enfield Creek and arrive at Lucifer
Falls, an impressive piece of natural sculpturing where
a waterfall tumbles 150 feet down a slanted rock face
between towering gorge walls.

The Enfield Glen is a post-glacial, water-eroded gorge
running through the heart of Tremen Park. While this
is not one of the larger gorges of the Finger Lakes
Region, it is a spectacular sight with walls 300 feet
high, falls, narrow passages, and chutes. There is also a
paved trail system that allows you to walk through the
gorge itself.

The section of the FLT described here has no official
name, but Enfield Trail seems appropriate, since the
village of Enfield is a short distance northeast of the
starting point and the trail crosses Enfield Creek at
the upper end of Enfield Glen in Tremen Park.

The upper end of the Enfield Glen gorge in Tremen Park

Access. The best approach to the trailhead follows
NY 13 south out of Ithaca for 3 miles to the
intersection with NY 327, which forks to the right.
Turn onto NY 327 and drive west 4.9 miles to the
intersection with Harvey Hill Road at Bostwick Corners.

Turn left (west) onto Harvey Hill Road and travel 2 miles
to the first intersection; turn left (south) on Black Oak
Road and drive 1 mile to Connecticut Hill Road.Turn
left (east) and drive another .8 mile, where Connecticut
Hill Road turns right (south) and Rumsey Hill Road
continues straight ahead (east). Park your car at the
corner, where you will see the white blazes of the FLT.

Trail. Follow the blazes east, downhill along Rumsey
Hill Road for about 200 yards where the FLT turns onto
a farm road on your left. The road runs past a barn
(which sits about 25 yards off the road), across a field,
and onto an abandoned wagon trail canopied by trees.
At the barn and along this part of the FLT you have a
fine view of distant hills to your right (east); the first
ridge is Jersey Hill in the Danby Region just south
of Ithaca.

About ½ mile from Rumsey Hill Road, the FLT enters a
wooded area and then starts a moderate descent into a
gully. At the base of the slope is a small unnamed brook
which flows east for two miles to empty into Enfield
Creek. The FLT crosses the brook, then turns sharply
right and follows it southeast for about ¾ mile on
another abandoned wagon road, crossing a small
feeder stream en route. This is a most pleasant walk
through a wooded glen. The trail here is wide, and in
summer the brook murmurs gently as it flows through
the cool, green glen.

Soon you emerge from the glen onto Trumbull Hill
Road (paved). Turn left here and follow the white trail

markers down the road for about 100 yards. Here the
trail turns right into a wooded area, and a few more
steps bring you to the brook you were following earlier.

The trail crosses the brook and heads uphill for about
150 yards, where it turns onto still another abandoned
wagon road. The trail is relatively flat, following the
contour of a hill that rises on your right, and it takes
you through a wooded area and a pleasant evergreen
stand. Through the woods to your left are fields, and
from time to time you encounter clearings that allow
you to look northeast over rolling farmland to another
range of hills.

From Trumbull Hill Road it is only ½ mile to Porter Hill
Road. Here again you will be treated to a fine view of
the countryside to the north and east.

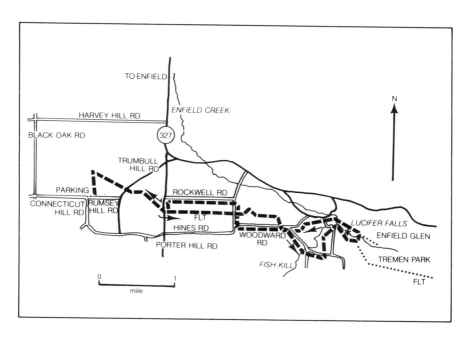

Cross Porter Hill Road and follow the markers into a small wooded area, then continue on a straight easterly course. You pass alternately through some open area and small wooded sections until you reach Hines Road 1 mile east of Porter Hill Road. The trail crosses Hines Road and follows a hedgerow bordering fields to your left and right before reaching the edge of a wooded area. It then edges the woods, gradually swinging southeast until it reaches Woodward Road (dirt).

Turn left on Woodward Road. After a short distance the trail forks right onto another, unmarked dirt road. The white trail blazes take you down this road 500 yards to a bridge which crosses Fish Kill, a clean, attractive stream that flows into Enfield Creek at the upper end of Tremen Park. Follow the FLT across the bridge to a dirt road about 100 feet beyond. Turn left on this road and walk to the top of a hill where the trail enters the woods on your right to follow a high rim overlooking Fish Kill. There is a clear view here to the northwest.

Follow the trail through the evergreens and hardwoods until you emerge on yet another abandoned road. As you step on the road you are leaving Tremen Park. Turn left and within a short distance a sign on you left tells you that you have again re-entered Tremen State Park.

The FLT follows this road as it bends sharply to the right and heads southeast. About 250 yards from the bend, the FLT forks right and heads uphill. It is at this junction that you stop following the FLT. Instead, continue straight ahead on the abandoned road another 200 yards as it runs eastward through a pleasant hardwood area where the trees canopy the road to an intersection with a paved footpath.

This is one of the park's hiking trails, built and maintained by the state. Turn right and in a short distance you come to your first overlook, with a view east into the gorge.

Continue a short distance to the second overlook. Here you can view Lucifer Falls head-on from the south rim. The drop to the circular plunge pool at the base of the falls is about 300 feet. During the spring when the creek waters are high, the sight is impressive.
A short walk beyond this overlook brings you to stone stairs, which take you down into the gorge to a footbridge across Enfield Creek. On the other side is Gorge Trail. Turn left here and follow this trail along the edge of the gorge back to Lucifer Falls for still another, but closer, view of the falls.

The footpath then takes you past several smaller falls, back over the creek and into the Upper Picnic Area, a pleasant spot to rest and have lunch. Follow the road out of the park a short distance to Woodward Road; another 150 yards along that brings you to the point where you turned off earlier to reach Fish Kill.

You now can return to your vehicle via Woodward Road, turning right onto Hines Road and then left on Rockwell Road to the FLT, which takes you to Trumbull Hill Road. Turn left on Trumbull Hill Road and then right onto Rumsey Hill Road to your vehicle.

Winter activities. Most of the route can be skied or snowshoed, with the exception of the Gorge Trail. The land is high and snowfall is good during January and February. Keep in mind that there are brooks to cross and some moderate climbing. Otherwise, ski touring is excellent.

21

Taughannock Falls State Park

Hiking distance: 4¼ miles
Hiking time: 2½ hours
Map: USGS Ludlowville

This short 4¼-mile hike takes you around and into an impressively deep gorge where the most striking attraction is Taughannock Falls. Plunging 215 feet into a 30-foot-deep pool, this falls is 55 feet higher than Niagara Falls. In fact it is one of the highest in the eastern United States. In the spring when the waters from melting snow rush into the upper end of the gorge and plunge over the crest, the falls becomes an awesome and breath-taking spectacle. Standing at the base, dwarfed by 400-foot walls that form an immense amphitheater, you may find yourself swept up in the beauty and grandeur of Taughannock Falls State Park.

There are several versions of the origin of the name "Taughannock" (pronounced Tau-han-nok). According to one account the name originated with the Indian word "Taghkanic," meaning "the great fall in the woods." A more interesting legend ties the name to a Taughannock chieftain of the Delaware tribes, which controlled the lands southeast of the Finger Lakes Region into Pennsylvania. The chieftain, who had been forced to relinquish claim to certain lands, led a band of warriors on a mission of revenge against the Cayugas. The mission was ill-fated; the chieftain fell in battle and his body was hurled into the gorge near the falls, which have born the name Taughannock ever since.

Taughannock Falls plunging 215 feet to the pool below

Though a bit less dramatic, the geological origin of the falls makes an interesting story, too. The rock layer that forms the base of the gorge and the stream bed of Taughannock Creek is Tully limestone, a hard, enduring mineral. The walls of the lower gorge are all black Geneseo shale, which has a crumbly composition. During the post-glacial period, the water quickly eroded this rock, washing it downstream to Lake Cayuga to form a large delta which is now the site of the North Point and South Point sections of the state park. Water erosion of the Geneseo shale halted in the lower gorge when the Tully limestone was reached, and in the middle of the gorge when Sherburne sandstone was exposed. The sections of harder rock that were not eroded eventually stood high above the lower stream bed, and Taughannock Falls was born.

Your hiking is done on a trail system located in the 825-acre Taughannock Falls State Park. The trails that run along both rims of the gorge are known respectively as the North Rim Trail and the South Rim Trail. A third trail, the Gorge Trail, runs from the parking lot at the lower end of the gorge to the foot of Taughannock Falls. There, on the north side of Taughannock Creek, a specially constructed observation area permits you to view the falls head-on.

Access. To reach your starting point at the upper end of the gorge, take NY 96 north from Ithaca or south from Waterloo to the village of Jacksonville. In the center of the village, turn north onto Jacksonville Road and drive 1.8 miles to the bridge over Taughannock Creek. Park your vehicle in the area on the south side of the bridge.

Trail. Walk across the bridge and pick up the foot trail on your right. It runs up a small embankment and into a clump of trees. A few feet into the trees you will see a footbridge. (Note: just before you cross the road bridge you encounter a sign reading Trail on the left. It points to a self-guided nature trail that runs along the south side of Taughannock Creek. You can obtain a printed guide to it from the park office at the lower end of the gorge.)

Walk to the middle of the footbridge. To your right (southwest) the water of Taughannock Creek plummets 100 feet down a sloping caprock into a plunge pool. This marks the beginning of the upper gorge system. To your left (northeast) the gorge becomes deeper, with walls that rise 200 feet straight up from the gorge floor.

Retrace your steps to the trail and follow it to the right (northeast) alongside Falls Road (paved) for ½ mile to a parking area. To your right, two observation points have been constructed to give you excellent head-on views of Taughannock Falls. The topmost vantage point is level with the parking area; the other is lower and somewhat closer to the falls.

You can now start your hike on the North Rim Trail, which begins at the east end of this parking area and affords you some fine views directly into the gorge. The trail pitches gradually downhill; near the end its slope is more pronounced, and it brings you out of the woods onto NY 89. Across the highway a picnic area fronts on Cayuga Lake. This is the delta of eroded Geneseo shale mentioned earlier.

Turn right onto the highway and walk over the bridge that crosses Taughannock Creek. Look upstream to the wide rock formation that forms a small falls. Continue another 200 feet to a parking area for the lower gorge on your right. You are now ready to follow the ¾-mile long Gorge Trail. Signs point the way. The gorge is quite wide here and so is the tree-shaded trail. As you walk toward the falls, you pass through a stand of trees; the base of the gorge now narrows and then widens again. On your left you will notice the piles of crumbly Geneseo shale along the side of the gorge wall.

As you near the falls, the trail turns right and crosses a footbridge, taking you to an observation platform where you can look directly at the falls and plunge pool.

After you have taken in the spectacular sight, retrace your steps to parking area on NY 89. Here you can easily find the South Rim Trail for the return route to your vehicle. Starting at the base, the trail ascends sharply through the woods to the gorge rim. From here

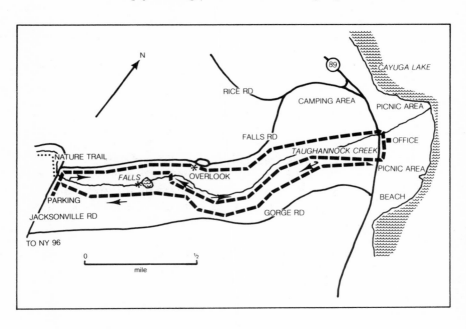

on the trail is relatively flat. Like the North Rim Trail, it runs along the edge of the gorge, allowing you to look down 400 feet to the floor.

One-quarter mile from the trail's end on Jacksonville Road you come to the spot where you can look directly down on the falls. The crest is 200 feet below; the plunge pool is 251 feet below the crest. It is an unusual and exciting vantage point.

Winter activities. The Gorge Trail and most of the upper portions of the rim trails can be skied or snowshoed. However, a better and safer alternative is the network of marked cross-country trails found in the northeast section of the park. This network runs from NY 89 through the camping area and across Rice Road, ending at the upper park entrance on Jacksonville Road. The return trip allows you to run downhill most of the way. There is also a recently constructed downhill ski slope near the camping area.

22

Hector Land Use Area

Hiking distance: 6½ miles
Hiking time: 3 hours
Maps: USGS Burdett; USGS Lodi

The Hector area is a delightful paradox. Its official name is the Hector Land Use Area. This pedestrian name, however, belies its true nature. It is a beautiful forested area sprinkled with more than a dozen sparkling wildlife ponds. One is tempted to call it wilderness, since it has the quality of the dense green Adirondack forests, yet this eleven-mile-long tract is surrounded by land where virtually every foot is under cultivation and where you find a mixture of dairy farms, fruit farms, and seemingly endless miles of vineyards. To drive from these rich farmlands into the Hector forest is a pleasantly startling transition.

Hector's 13,000 acres lie astride a relatively flat ridge running from Burdett and Bennettsburg near the south end of Seneca Lake to Lodi in the north. Yet this flatness is deceptive, for Hector occupies high ground with elevations exceeding 1,800 feet, giving you excellent views to the east and west. The land pitches sharply down on both sides of the ridge to the lakes, where the elevations are less than 400 feet—a vertical drop of more than 1,400 feet in just a few miles.

Hector is one of the largest parcels of federally owned land in New York state, a fact not too many New Yorkers know. It is under the jurisdiction of the Forest Service of the U.S. Department of Agriculture, and is adminstered by the staff of the Forest Service's Green Mountain National Forest in neighboring Vermont.

All this makes the area unusual, but most unusual—from a hiker's point of view—is Hector's system of broad, blazed, and well-maintained trails, all marked by signs reading No Motorized Vehicles Allowed. Running north and south down the broad back of the ridge is a section of the 25-mile-long Interloken Trail, which, as the name implies, locks a network of spur trails and loops with the Finger Lake Trail (FLT) that crosses the southern end of this national forest land.

Extending from the Interloken Trail are such attractive hiking routes as the Backbone, Potomac, Ravine, Burnt Hill, Gorge, and Southslope trails. Camping areas found in the forest are the Blueberry Patch Recreation Site and Potomac Campgrounds, and at the south end just off the Finger Lakes Trail, a lean-to.

Looking out over one of the wildlife ponds in the Hector Land Use Area

The hike suggested here is a sampler. It is relatively short, but one which allows you in one loop to get the feel of several trails, specifically sections of the Finger Lakes, Interloken, and Burnt Hill trails and all of the Southslope and Gorge trails.

Access. Take NY 414 north out of Watkins Glen or south out of Seneca Falls. A mile north of Watkins Glen turn northeast onto NY 79/NY 227, which runs through Burdett en route to Bennettsburg. Follow this route past Burdett for .8 mile to Logan Road (County Route 4). Turn north onto Logan Road and drive 1.1 miles to Wycoff Road, a dirt road on your right. Turn here and drive uphill for .4 mile to Burnt Hill Road. Turn left (north) and continue on Burnt Hill Road past a sign on the right that tells you that you have entered the Hector Land Use Area. Shortly you reach a sign for the Finger Lakes Trail, which here enters the woods on your right. Leave your vehicle several hundred feet further along in a parking area on your left.

Trail. Walk north on the road for 100 feet to another sign for the Finger Lakes Trail. This time the sign points to a trail entering the woods on your left. Here is where you begin your hike.

Turn onto the white-blazed FLT and follow it as it heads northwest, descending gradually. Soon the downhill pitch becomes more pronounced, and the trail dips sharply into a gully, crosses a brook, and heads up the embankment of the other side. About ½ mile from your starting point on Burnt Hill Road the trail forks and a sign tells you that South-slope Trail goes to the right. Following the sign for the Southslope Trail, bear right. This trail is marked with orange blazes. Only ¼ mile long, it runs in an arc that brings you back onto Burnt Hill Road. Cross the road and follow the path along the south (dam) end of a small but attractive wildlife pond. On the far side you intersect the north-south Interloken Trail, also blazed orange.

Turn left onto the Interloken Trail and head north for little over ¼ mile past another wildlife pond to Burnt Hill Road again. Here the trail turns sharply to the right and re-enters the woods. A sign reading Recreation Area points you in the correct direction.

The Interloken Trail heads east a short distance, then north, and finally east again. About ¼ mile from Burnt Hill Road you encounter another set of signs which inform you that the Interloken Trail bears left (north) and the Gorge Trail continues straight. Take the Gorge Trail, which soon crosses a small wooden footbridge spanning a slight depression and a trickle of water. This small depression quickly deepens into a gully which, in turn, becomes a ravine. The trail meanders

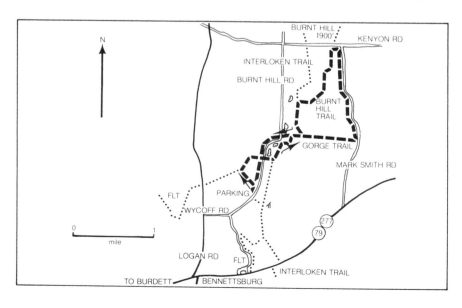

through an attractive section of the woods on the north edge of the cut, allowing you to observe how gorges develop. Near the trail's end, a sizable drop yawns on your right, with almost vertical sides reaching the gorge floor several hundred feet below.

The Gorge Trail ends at Mark Smith Road, a single dirt lane. Turn left (north) here and follow it uphill. The road is tree-lined and generally shaded, making it a pleasant walk. Near the top the land flattens out and walking becomes easier as you approach Kenyon Road. From the end of the Gorge Trail to Kenyon Road, the distance is just a mile.

At Kenyon Road you have a fine view to the east. Turn left and follow Kenyon Road a short distance to the crest of Burnt Hill (el. 1,900'), one of the highest spots in the Hector area. Here, too, you will see a sign pointing to the southern leg of the Burnt Hill Trail, which crosses Kenyon Road.

Take this trail and head south. It is flat and meanders through the woods, snaking south, west, south and finally arcing west again until it intersects the Interloken Trail. The walk from Kenyon Road to the Interloken Trail is just short of a mile.

Follow the Interloken Trail to a short spur trail on your right (to the east this becomes the Gorge Trail). This spur takes you past another wildlife pond to Burnt Hill Road. Turn left (south) on the road and little over a mile brings you back to your vehicle.

Winter activities. The whole Hector area is ideal for snowshoeing and ski touring. The wooded areas hold the snow well and the trail system is extensive enough to allow you to select loops of varying length. In general, however, the trails are flat.

23
Sugar Hill
State Forest

Hiking distance: 5 miles
Hiking time: 2½ hours
Maps: USGS Reading Center; USGS Wayne

October is the best time to hike at Sugar Hill. The air is cool, the sky is clear, and the autumn foliage for which the area is famous is at its peak. In fact, to walk Sugar Hill in the fall is to walk through a color explosion, for you are awash in waves of yellow, red, crimson, gold, blue and purple as the sunlight streams in from all sides through beeches, oaks, hickories, maples, and ashes. It is an experience that will sharpen your senses and quicken your spirit.

The trail system here is ideally designed to allow you to take in the richness of the season. You will pass through hardwood stands, down tree-lined lanes, and across deserted farmlands that have now become the territory of saplings and young trees. A network of roads makes access to all of the trails easy, and the choices open to the hiker are almost unlimited.

Sugar Hill State Forest covers 9,085 acres of hill country between the southern tip of Seneca Lake in the east and Waneta Lake and Lameka Lake in the west. Atop the area's highest point on the northern edge of the state forest is the Sugar Hill Recreational Area, a state-operated site where you can picnic, camp, and climb a fire tower for a spectacular view of the rugged hill country to the south. There is an archery range nearby, and trails for hikers and horseback riders radiate out from the parking lot.

There is a spectacular view from atop the fire tower in the Sugar Hill Recreation Area

Access. The hike recommended here begins on County Route 21 about .6 mile south of Tower Hill Road at the point where the Finger Lakes Trail (FLT) crosses. This puts you within easy reach of three lean-tos and offers you some fine overlooks facing east toward Seneca Lake.

To reach your starting point, take County Route 28 west out of Watkins Glen (located on the southern tip of Seneca Lake). About a mile out of town, County Route 28 runs into County Route 23; fork left onto County Route 23 and drive about 6 miles until you see a sign on the right directing you to turn left for the Sugar Hill Recreational Area.

This turn puts you on County Route 21. Drive south for 1 mile to cross Tower Hill Road. From Tower Hill Road, you continue for .6 mile to where an abandoned road crosses County Route 21. Park here, for the abandoned road is a section of the FLT (blazed white) on which you will begin your hike.

Trail. Start your hike by walking east on the abandoned road, identified on the USGS map as Sickler Road. Although it doubles as a horse trail, no motorized vehicles are allowed.

The road is tree-lined for part of the way, but it soon becomes more open as you pass through fields where saplings and small trees have just begun to take over. After about ¼ mile, a trail marker points to your left (north). Turn here and follow the FLT as it crosses another abandoned field, dips into a gully, and passes through a wooded area. The trail soon turns right (east) and crosses aspen stands, wooded areas, and more abandoned fields until it brings you to the first of the three lean-tos.

There is an old, unused wagon road behind the lean-to;
it swings north and offers an alternate route by which
you can return to County Route 21. Your hike, however,
continues on the FLT, which passes in front of the
lean-to, taking you southeast through some open areas
and back into the forest on some high ground. Watch
on your left for the deep cut formed by Glen Creek—the
creek which eventually flows into the deep Watkins
Glen Gorge, some 3 miles to the east. In this area the
cut is known as Van Zandt Hollow.

The FLT follows the western edge of the hollow until it
encounters a feeder stream. Here it turns right (west)
for a short distance, crosses the stream at a low spot,
and heads back in an easterly direction to Sickler Road.

At this point, the FLT turns left (east) toward Watkins
Glen. Your route, however, follows Sickler Road to the
right (west), heading uphill through a wooded area. You
soon cross an open stretch and pass the point where

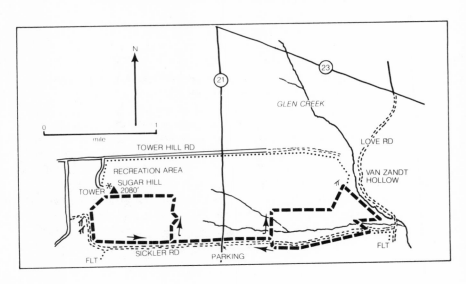

you earlier turned off Sickler Road. A short walk brings you back to your vehicle.

You may stop now, but the recommended hike continues west on Sickler Road (which is also the FLT here) for about ¼ mile through a heavily wooded area. Remain on the FLT when it turns off to your right (north) to climb toward the recreational area at the top of Sugar Hill (el. 2,080').

The fire tower atop Sugar Hill offers you some striking views of the surrounding landscape. You may wish to stop here for lunch or a rest before you return to the FLT and continue your hike downhill past two more lean-tos and a horse barn.

You now find yourself back on Sickler Road. Bear left (south). After ¼ mile the road curves left (east), but the FLT continues straight on a southerly course. Remain on Sickler Road and walk eastward for about 1 mile to return to County Route 21 and your vehicle.

Winter activities. This area is actively used during the winter months by snowmobilers and ski tourers. The suggested hiking trail is particularly suited for ski touring, for it crosses varied terrain, adding zest and challenge to a fine day's skiing. The snow is plentiful here, and it packs well in the forest area and on the trails, providing excellent ski conditions during January, February, and March.

24
Gannett Hill

Hiking distance: 11 miles
Hiking time: 5 hours
Map: USGS Bristol Springs

This hike takes you through the magnificent mountainous country just west of the southern tip of Canandaigua Lake—an area variously known as the Bristol Hill region, the Gannett Hill section, and New York's Italian Alps.

"Mountainous" may be a bit of an overstatement. These "mountains" are no match for the European Alps, the western Rockies, or even the high peaks of the Adirondacks. Carved by glacial activity during the Pleistocene period, they are technically only hills, as they barely top out at 2,200 feet. But when you hike this region your senses insist that you are surrounded by mountains. From a distance rugged, straight-shouldered, tree-covered hulks dominate narrow valleys. And when you are on top of one of these hills, the world drops away at your feet with breath-taking suddenness, revealing spectacular views of the gorge-like valleys below.

Although the hills hereabouts do have an alpine appearance, you might well wonder why they are called "Italian." First, there are the local place names—Naples, Naples Creek, Italy Hill, and Italy Valley. Second, this is fine wine country. Vineyards grace the valleys and lower hill sections surrounding the village of Naples, the site of a major winery and hub of the local wine industry.

The hike starts in Ontario County Park on the top of Gannett Hill, the highest point in this region. Here you are at the northern end of a spur trail of the Finger Lakes Trail (FLT) system, the Bristol Hill Branch Trail. This trail, which is blazed orange, runs south almost thirty miles to Mitchellsville (just north of Bath), where it meets the main east-west Finger Lakes Trail. The hike described here, however, only uses part of the Bristol Hill Branch Trail, following it along the Gannett Hill ridge and then over Cleveland Hill to a dirt road. There you leave the trail and return to your start in the county park by way of dirt roads that run over Powell Hill and along the eastern edge of Gannett Hill. Since you do some hill climbing, this hike is best classified as moderate to difficult.

Mist shrouds the Gannett Hill ridge opposite the Jumpoff

Access. You can reach Ontario County Park by following NY 21 north out of Naples for 6 miles to Bristol Springs. In this hamlet turn left onto NY 64 and continue .5 mile north to Gannett Hill Road. Turn left and drive 1.5 miles to the park. There is a modest entry fee for your vehicle; a brochure and map of the park are also available at the entrance (or you can obtain them in advance by writing: Division of Human Services, Ontario County, Canandaigua, NY 14424).

Leave your vehicle in the area near the sign pointing to the Jumpoff and walk the short distance to this overlook. The Jumpoff is aptly named; once you reach the overlook there is nothing but daylight between you and the valley floor 800 feet below.

Trail. Beginning at the Jumpoff, your route follows the FLT spur trail to the left along the edge of the hill for about 100 yards, giving you an excellent view of the valley below, West Hollow to the south, and Berby Hollow to the north. It then swings left, taking you into the woods and onto the flatter land of the Gannet Hill ridge. It soon drops into a gully and then moves uphill for a little more than ¼ mile before again leveling out. At this point you are just to the right of Gannett Hill's summit, which at 2,256 feet is the highest point in the Bristol Hill region.

After another ¼ mile of relatively level walking, you begin a ½-mile descent into West Hollow. At the base of the hill, on level ground again, you pass an area used for tenting by hikers and soon break out of the woods into an open field. The trail now swings right (west) and in ¼ mile emerges on West Hollow Road (paved).

Cross the highway, turn right, and walk a short distance down the road until you pick up the Cleveland

Hill section of the trail on your left, designated by a sign and orange trail markers. Once in the woods, you start uphill; the climb is steep and demanding, requiring you to make a 400-foot ascent in less than ½ mile. As you near the summit of Cleveland Hill, the land flattens considerably, and for almost 1 mile you walk the relatively level north-south ridge, passing over the crest (el. 2,200') at midpoint.

When the trail eventually begins to descend Cleveland Hill's south side, it does so gradually. Over the next ½ mile, however, the slope becomes more pronounced, and the final pitch before the base is quite sharp. When you reach the bottom the trail leads you across an open field (used by Scouts as a camping area) to a jeep trail that brings you to a dirt road.

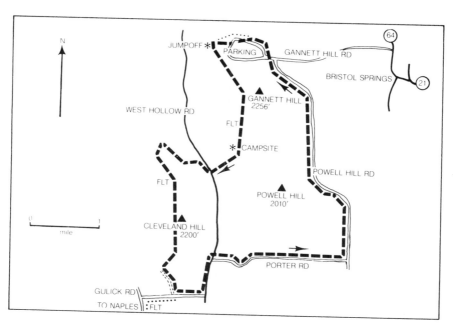

Here you leave the Bristol Hill Branch Trail. Turn left (east) and walk the short distance to West Hollow Road. Turn left again and continue north on this road for ½ mile until you come to Porter Road. Turn right onto this dirt road, which runs east through the flatland of West Hollow. Because of the open fields on both sides of the road, you have an excellent view of High Point Hill and Cleveland Hill to the west and Powell Hill to the north.

In 1½ miles you reach Powell Hill Road. Again you turn left and walk north. The first ½ mile is over level ground. Then the road begins to rise as it bends westward, coming gradually up the east side of Powell Hill. Another ½-mile walk brings you to the summit (el. 2,000'). To the east you have a grand view of the Naples Creek Valley and Canandaigua Lake beyond. The road now levels out, making the 3-mile walk back to Ontario County Park and your vehicle relatively easy.

The park also boasts an excellent network of well-marked trails that tie into the southbound Finger Lakes branch trail and would make a good base for a weekend outing. A number of campsites are available for overnight camping.

Winter activities. Once the snow comes, it packs well and stays a long time. However, although sections on the flatlands and valleys are ideal for cross-country skiing, generally this is not the place for touring; the trails are a bit too steep to negotiate with Nordic skis. On the other hand, snowshoeing here can be fun, particularly along the Bristol Hill Branch Trail.

25
Hornell-Canisteo Area

Hiking distance: 10¼ miles
Hiking time: 5 hours
Map: USGS Canisteo

There comes a time when a hiker wants to see the world in a special way—to walk the hilltops where the view is unobstructed, to look down long valleys that radiate from hills like spokes on a wheel, to see the soft blue of the hills and ridges far beyond, and to sense the openness of the high country all around. If you feel this way sometime, try the section of the Finger Lakes Trail (FLT) in the Hornell-Canisteo area on the western side of the Finger Lakes Region, for this region has a grandeur that sets it apart from the rest of the state.

The hills here are a major attraction. They are tall (many exceed 2,000 feet in elevation), but they tend to be rounded on top and circular at the base. Of particular interest to hikers is the fact that many of the hilltops continue to be farmed, mostly for hay, allowing you unobstructed views of the landscape on all sides. Even on rainy or misty days the panoramas can be exhilarating. The entire region is classified as Appalachian Upland, and you will be hiking through the uplands eastern section, called the Cattaraugus Hills.

This is also great fossil country. Virtually any outcrop will offer you an abundant selection of Devonian fossils, usually brachiopods and trilobites. You may find them in the stony hillsides as well as in the stream beds of gullies and ravines.

Access. This hiking area is most easily approached from the rest of the state by way of Howard on NY 70. Leave NY 70 at the Howard interchange and turn south to enter the town. Continue through town, driving south on County Route 27 for 3 miles to County Route 109 (Turnpike Road). Head west on this road for 1.3 miles to Woods Road, the first dirt road on your left. Turn here and drive south for .3 mile to Burt Hill Road, which forks right. Drive along Burt Hill Road for .3 mile and park.

Hikers head into the woods on the white-blazed Finger Lakes Trail

Trail. The spot where you have parked is located atop some of the highest land in the area (el. 2,140'), and the view is breath-taking. Burt Hill Road runs along the crest of a ridge, and because the surrounding land is not forested, you can drink in the magnificent scenery as you walk. Begin your hike by walking south on Burt Hill Road for 1 ¼ miles to Windfall Hill Road, the first dirt road on your right.

Turn right and walk downhill for about 100 yards. On your right in a small clump of trees look for a white blaze painted on a tree to indicate the entrance to the FLT. Before you turn onto the FLT, look down Windfall Hill Road to enjoy still another fine view of the hills between you and the town of Hornell, four miles away.

Climb the embankment on your right and follow the FLT into the woods. The trail takes you north past a field on your left that allows you to continue to enjoy the spectacular scenery.

Before long, the trail begins a slow descent, heading left across the corner of a field and into another wooded area. Soon you are following a small gully on your left that gradually deepens to become a respectable ravine. You pass through a pleasant, well-spaced stand of hemlocks just before the trail pitches downward again for a short distance and enters a level section of woods. There are large pines in this area that, judging from their size, are probably 75 to 100 years old. Most of the trees in this vicinity are tall and thick, indicating that little lumbering has been done here in the last century.

So far the hike has been a gradual descent from the hilltop where you parked your car. You are at the bottom now, and ahead you see Cunningham Creek

flowing south on its way to the Canisteo River. The
trail follows the creek a short distance and then
crosses it, bringing you onto a dirt road. Turn left and
follow the road south past a beef cattle farm for ½ mile.
White blazes are painted on trees to guide you along
this part of the FLT. Just as you reach a bridge over
Cunningham Creek you see double white blazes on a
tree on your right, signalling you to turn right.

The trail begins a moderately steep ascent, moving
through a wooded area along the edge of a gully on
your right. After about ¼ mile you leave the woods and
enter a field. You continue uphill along the forest's
edge, and another ¼ mile brings you to the crest of the
hill. To your left is a line of fence posts; about every
third one bears a white blaze, indicating the direction
of the trail. Turn left and follow the posts, keeping
them on your right.

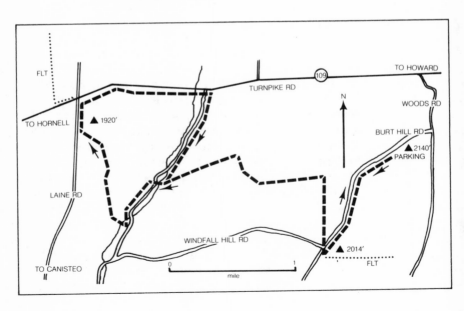

Again you have a grand view to the east and the north, and again valleys seem to radiate in all directions. It is delightful scenery, so walk slowly and enjoy it.

On the far side of the fence, ahead and to the right, you will see a small house. Soon you are abreast of it, and a few more steps bring you to Laine Road (dirt). Turn right and follow it for about 200 yards to meet County Route 109 (Turnpike Road), the paved east-west road you drove earlier. Turn right and walk east on this road for just over 1 mile to an unmarked dirt road leading off on your right (south).

You have reached another high spot, and you have an excellent view of valleys and distant hills to the north and west.

Turn right (south) on the unmarked dirt road. This is a pleasant downhill walk alongside Cunningham Creek, and in about ¾ mile you are back at the section of the FLT which you walked earlier. Turn left onto the FLT, cross Cunningham Creek, and head back uphill to your starting point. When you reach your vehicle, pause once more to gaze over this remarkable landscape.

Winter activities. This area is relatively poor for ski touring or snowshoeing; there are too many steep hills, and the snow is not as plentiful here as in other parts of the Finger Lakes Region. The snow that does fall is generally blown off the exposed hilltops.

Guidebooks from New Hampshire Publishing Company

Written for people of all ages and experience, these highly popular and carefully prepared books feature detailed trail directions, notes on points of interest, sketch maps, and photographs.

For *New York* state—

Discover the Adirondacks 1: From Indian Lake to the Hudson River/A Four-Season Guide
Barbara McMartin. $6.95

25 Walks in the Finger Lakes Region
Bill Ehling. $5.95

In the *Fifty Hikes* series—

Fifty Hikes in Central Pennsylvania
Tom Thwaites. $6.95

Fifty Hikes in Vermont
Ruth and Paul Sadlier. $6.95

Fifty Hikes in Connecticut
Gerry and Sue Hardy. $6.95

Fifty Hikes in Massachusetts
Paul and Ruth Sadlier. $6.95

Fifty More Hikes in New Hampshire
Daniel Doan. $6.95

Fifty Hikes in the White Mountains
Daniel Doan. $6.95

Fifty Hikes in Maine
John Gibson. $6.95

Other guides—

20 Bicycle Tours in Vermont
John S. Freidin. $5.95

25 Ski Tours in Western Massachusetts
John Frado, Richard Lawson, and Robert Coy. $4.95

25 Ski Tours in the Green Mountains
Sally and Daniel Ford. $4.95

Canoe Camping Vermont and New Hampshire Rivers
Roioli Schweiker. $4.95

Available from bookstores, sporting goods stores, or the publisher.
For complete descriptions of these and other guides in the **25 Walks**, **Canoeing**, **25 Ski Tours**, and **Bicycle Tours** series, write:
New Hampshire Publishing Company, Box 70, Somersworth, NH 03878.